The Meaning of Life.
A Quick Immersion

Quick Immersions provide illuminating introductions to diverse topics in the worlds of social science, the hard sciences, philosophy and the humanities. Written in clear and straightforward language by prestigious authors, the texts also offer valuable insights to readers seeking a deeper knowledge of those fields.

Predrag Cicovacki

THE MEANING OF LIFE
A Quick Immersion

Tibidabo Publishing
New York

Copyright © 2021 by Predrag Cicovacki

Published by Tibidabo Publishing, Inc. New York.

All rights reserved. No part of this publication may be reproduced, stored in a retrieval system, or transmitted, in any form or by any means, electronic, mechanical, photocopying, recording, scanning or otherwise, without the prior permission in writing with the Publisher or as permitted by law, or under terms agreed upon with the appropriate reprographics rights organization.

Copyediting by Lori Gerson
Cover art by Raimon Guirado

First published 2021

Visit our Series on our Web:
www.quickimmersions.com

ISBN: 978-1-949845-28-0
1 2 3 4 5 6 7 8 9 10

Library of Congress Control Number: 2021943309

Printed in the United States of America.

"For thousands of years we have gathered in circle –
around fires, around bodies, around altars –
because we can't do this alone."
–Wayne Muller

Contents

Introduction	9
1. Merit	20
2. Luck	46
3. Gratitude	82
4. Inspiration	118
Closing Thoughts	158
Further Reading	164

Introduction

There comes a time when each of us is overwhelmed by life's demands. Whether the reasons are subjective, as in cases of personal failures or misfortunes, or objective, as when our environment is stricken by social turmoil or a deadly pandemic, we stop functioning on an instinctual autopilot. Instead of: How do I go on?, the question becomes: Why should I go on? This reversal may even lead us to face the terrifying prospect that all life may be futile: Why are we here? Does it make any meaningful difference whether we exist or not?

Confronted with such challenges, we may still want to continue life's struggle, but only if it offers some reasonable hope for a positive outcome. We love life and treat it as valuable, but we also realize that there are things we love and value more than life. Most of us similarly hate death; there are things, however, we hate more than death and, in some circumstances, death is welcomed.

This reasonable and humane approach to life may have first been advocated by the Chinese philosopher Mencius, more than two thousand years ago. Mencius realized that human beings have similar hopes and aspirations, joys and sorrows; feelings of mercy and respect are present in all of us, as are the senses of pride and shame, right and wrong. Such feelings establish our essential equality. These insights led Mencius to maintain that there is something like the "common heart" of humanity. All of us have this heart, but only some are able to preserve and nourish it. That is how we become different from each other.

To use these insights of Mencius as the basis for our thinking about the meaning of life, we must make four preliminary remarks. First, the meaning of life should be discussed only in the context of relationships with others. Philosophers often scrutinize the lonely figure of Sisyphus who had to roll a huge rock to the top of a mountain, from which it always tumbled down. Separated from all living creatures, Sisyphus lived with his rock, as lonely as the rock and just as aimless. The story of Sisyphus may be so appealing to our age because we live increasingly disconnected and lonely lives. And this is not because we are forcefully separated from other living beings, as Sisyphus was, but because we have misused or neglected our "common heart." That heart exists to connect us with other living beings, for we can flourish only through our engaged participation in the cycles of life and in circles with others.

Second, when we pursue the riddle of life's meaning, we should keep in mind that we are dealing with living organisms, not dead things. Because our lives consist increasingly in serving machines and having their efficiency as our standard of work, we organize our lives as if we were machines. But machines we are not, nor do we do ourselves a favor when we imitate them. Machines are cold and unfeeling, while we are warm and sensitive. We are living beings, whose functioning cannot be mechanically programmed and maintained. For better or worse, we are fluid and changing, emotional and temperamental, imaginative and unpredictable.

Third, we are discussing the meaning of *human* life. We can talk about the lives of mosquitos and earthworms and wonder why such creatures exist in the first place, or we can puzzle over the display of emotions and apparently intelligent behavior of our cats and dogs. But our puzzlement is specifically about the meaning of human life and the qualities and values that bestow meaning on our lives. Mencius spoke about the common human heart, which includes not only our moral reasoning and sentiments but also our emotions and aspirations.

Plato, who was a contemporary of Mencius, used the word "soul" instead of "heart" to advocate a similar but more elaborate view. For Plato, the three parts of the immaterial soul in the physical body are reason (enabling the person to perform rationally), spirit (accounting for anger, ambition, a sense of honor, etc.), and the appetites (desires for food, drink, and sex). Excellence in the performance of these functions represent the virtues of wisdom, courage, and temperance, respectively; and when all are present, the virtue of justice is present. Plato maintained that in each of us, one of the three parts is more dominant than the other two. That the most dominant part of our soul, rather than our individual inclinations or social respectability, should be decisive in our choice of life-calling. When each of these parts performs its natural function and does not interfere with the work of the other two, the soul can achieve a harmonious existence—in every individual and in society as a whole. Somewhat surprisingly, Plato calls this justice rather than harmony. But we should keep in mind that, for Plato, justice is the symbol of a harmonious and virtuous life. It is also, we can add, a symbol of a meaningful life.

Fourth, some lives are more meaningful than others. Although both Mencius and Plato were preoccupied with what it means for any human being—Chinese or Greek, man or woman, wealthy or poor, educated or not— to live a meaningful life, they each had a predecessor with extraordinary gifts and qualities who inspired them to recognize disparities in the degrees of meaningfulness; only a few become masters of the art of living. In the case of Mencius, the predecessor was Confucius. For Plato, it was Socrates. Having these examples led them to believe that the development of both our general human capacities and our unique gifts determines whether and to what degree our lives are meaningful. Although individualism did not emerge as a prominent ideology until at least the twelfth century—the era of the troubadours—and although we are currently preoccupied with our differences to the point that we have a hard time imagining any general human nature or qualities we may all have in common, the meaning of life must be considered from both perspectives: generally human and uniquely individual.

To approach this nuanced understanding of the meaning of life, our analysis of this topic will be divided into four chapters dealing with merit, luck, gratitude, and inspiration, respectively. Let us briefly anticipate what we will discuss concerning each of them.

Even a casual reflection on life leads us to recognize that it is organized around what can be called the principle of merit: we have to earn, or deserve, almost anything we want to accomplish. We are introduced to this principle in our childhood: to get ice cream after a meal, we have to eat the main dish, whether we like it or not. To get good grades, we need to study hard. To get a present from Santa Claus, we need to be good boys and girls throughout the year. Regardless how simplistic it may be, the same principle guides much of our adult life, regardless of whether we are thinking about getting a job, earning a promotion, or securing enough funds for a comfortable retirement. This principle introduces a workman-like attitude into our entire life and induces us to treat our lives as analogous to a workplace.

The principle of merit has been present in every culture and every age. It brings order and stability to our lives and seems, at least on the surface, to provide us unambiguous guidelines as to how to live meaningful lives. This principle can be summed up by using the metaphor of a dividing line: virtuousness leads to reward, while vice brings us punishment. Equally important, this principle reminds us that to a significant degree, even if not exclusively, it is up to us whether our lives will be good and enjoyable or bad and full of suffering. As Plato put it, leading virtuous lives should bring us to the gates of happiness.

Although the principle of merit provides a roadmap for our attempts to live meaningful lives, things are not always as fair as this principle requires them to be. We all know of numerous instances in which virtue does not seem to be rewarded and when vice is not punished. If we are religiously oriented, we may support this principle by believing that God sees and knows everything: if not in this life, then in another, virtue will be adequately repaid and vice castigated. Yet even those who believe in another life and God's justice recognize that there is something else that must be taken into account when thinking about the meaning of life: luck. Here, we can recognize another dividing line, just a different one from the line associated with merit. Some of us are lucky to be born with special gifts, while others are simply average—or below. Some are lucky to be raised in stable, loving, or wealthy families, and some are not. Some of us grow up in an open and prosperous society, while others live under oppressive or corrupt regimes. Some never experience war, while others may be sent to gas chambers. Furthermore, we may be lucky in one aspect of life but not so in another. Alternatively, while we may be lucky now, the wheel of fortune may quickly turn. Instead of life being fundamentally fair, as the principle of merit suggests, do not such examples show that much in life is due to sheer luck, rather than to hard work and moral discipline? Perhaps life is less like a workplace than a market—or a bazaar—at which we occasionally get a good bargain while at other times are cheated.

Merit and luck are both factors contributing to a meaningful life. They are also external factors, and it is easy to recognize that we often sacrifice some of our finer feelings and compromise internally important values for outside advantages. But being human requires that such internal factors also be taken into account. External factors may be indispensable for a meaningful life, but we cannot always control our external circumstances. We can influence our inner attitudes toward whatever life presents to us, however. All spiritual and religious traditions are built on this realization, as is much of philosophy. Socrates was sentenced to death, but he accepted his destiny with dignity and integrity; he spent his last day in jail not lamenting his punishment but discussing with his friends whether we can know that the human soul is immortal. Similarly, Confucius gracefully endured maltreatment from the local Chinese rulers. None of these rulers was willing to act on his instructions, but Confucius was convinced of the value of the way of life he was teaching. When arrested or detained, it was his habit to sing or recite poetry to self-accompaniment on a stringed instrument. Even under the most unfavorable circumstances, Confucius did not lose his composure, and he continued to develop his teaching. The power of inner strength should not be underestimated.

There is no one accepted name for such an internal attitude, nor is there agreement on its essential characteristics. Some describe it in terms of the contrast between manipulation and appreciation, or as the tension between the profane and the sacred. Some insist that it is personal integrity, some that it consists of peace of mind, and some argue in favor of happiness. Some emphasize the central role of feelings and, symbolically, of the heart; thus, they recognize it in love—whether love of God, brotherly love, love of friends, or personal love.

I will consider this inner attitude under the umbrella concept of gratitude. Gratitude may be more stable and permanent than either happiness or love; it is the subjective equivalent of the principle of merit. Gratitude is not characterized by a dividing line but is based on an attitude that connects. It involves two essential components that make it flexible enough to include the elements of both love and happiness: care and appreciation. For our lives to be meaningful, we need to care about something and someone and to care enough to appreciate the most diverse aspects of life. Georg Simmel called gratitude the "moral memory of humankind," but it is an attitude that is by no means limited to the moral realm: we can be grateful for a beautiful sunset, a hummingbird buzzing around blossoming flowers, or a well-performed musical composition. Furthermore, gratitude is directed as much to the future as it is to the past. Like an arched bridge slightly raised in the middle, gratitude gives us a slightly elevated perspective of reality. If such a perspective leads us toward appreciation of the most and seemingly disparate aspects of reality, it will incline us toward becoming warm-hearted and balanced human beings. Although Mencius and Plato did not explicitly discuss gratitude, I will argue that this idea covers and further clarifies much of their vision of a meaningful life.

To account for the relevance of our unique gifts and internal qualities, we also need to discuss what I call "inspiration." I take this idea in a double sense:

some individuals are inspired to accomplish great deeds and exceptional works, and some serve as an inspiration for others. Two of my inspirations are Albert Schweitzer and Antoni Gaudi. Schweitzer (1875-1965) abandoned his academic and artistic career to become a doctor in a part of Africa with high rates of malaria, where he spent close to five decades of his life. He also developed there his ethics of reverence for all forms of life.

Gaudi (1852-1926) created several divinely inspired works of architecture, culminating in the Sagrada Familia, in Barcelona. The foundation stone for this basilica was set in 1882, when Gaudi was only thirty-one years old, and it has not yet been completed. Gaudi conceived it as growing slowly, like an oak tree, so that, when fully grown, it can withstand the winds of change. This fascinating construction is almost entirely devoid of straight lines because Gaudi insisted that straight lines do not exist in nature and because he wanted to create something that would represent the manifestation of the divine in nature.

The lives and works of Gaudi and Schweitzer bring nature and spirit harmoniously together—a rare accomplishment in our civilization that is determined to keep them separate. Extraordinary personalities like Schweitzer and Gaudi change our understanding of the limits of what is humanly possible and inspire us to seek innovative forms of healing and harmonizing. Whether primarily intended for healing or prayer, celebration or mourning, the sanctuaries these individuals created bring us back together; they connect and inspire. They help us realize that, in addition to hard work and a bit of luck, nothing of great quality can be accomplished without sacrifice and enthusiasm, without bonding and sharing.

What, then, are the lessons we can learn from such great personalities? Perhaps the following two. First, theory and practice, ideas about life and ways of life should be inseparable. As talking about morality should not be detached from practicing virtue, discussing the meaning of life should not be separated from attempting to live as meaningfully as possible. Why else would we discuss the meaning of life? Second, these individuals teach us that living a meaningful life cannot ultimately be a mere quest for individual achievement or prosperity. The self is neither the ultimate reality, nor should it be our ultimate concern. Our quest for meaning must instead be oriented toward something that is greater than our individual lives, and what we need to discern is what are, and are not, proper objects of such devotion.

If they prove to be justified, such insights should enable us to answer the ultimate question regarding the meaning of life: Why are we here?

Chapter 1
Merit

Meaning versus Meaninglessness

There is hardly a child—or adult—who would not smile while reciting the verses:

> Humpty Dumpty sat on a wall,
> Humpty Dumpty had a great fall.
> All the king's horses and all the king's men
> Couldn't put Humpty together again.

What is so enjoyable about these seemingly meaningless words? And what makes this playful combination of words such that, once we learn it in childhood, we remember it with joy for the rest of our lives?

Before we can say what makes something meaningful, it may be easier to discern why something is meaningless. Two extreme cases come immediately to mind. A chaotic jumble of various elements—letters or sounds, things or happenings—is meaningless if the elements cannot be arranged to form a coherent picture or story; "a pattern that connects" seems to be a necessary presupposition for anything meaningful. But not just any pattern will do. Unlike the surprising pattern we discern in the nursery rhyme Humpty Dumpty, a rigidly and endlessly repetitive pattern can result in meaninglessness. The patterned but repetitive motions performed by Sisyphus, for example, reflect no pulsation of life but resemble the working of an automaton. Rolling a rock uphill for all eternity, only to have it fall back down to the bottom, cannot strike us as anything other than meaningless. Nor can a life of monotonous routine, if it is not filled with experiences of joy and love, or at least a clear sense of why the repeated performance of such colorless tasks is needed.

These extreme cases of meaninglessness reveal to us the conceptual space within which we can experience something as meaningful. The patterns we recognize in the verses of "Mother Goose" are rhymes. The lines of the poem rhyme, as does the name Humpty Dumpty. Taken by themselves, "Humpty" and "Dumpty" are meaningless words.

A pattern formed by mere repetition of one of them would provide a sense of regularity, but sheer quantity of repetitions would not bring any qualitative meaning. Neither Humpty Humpty, nor Dumpty Dumpty works, but Humpty Dumpty does, although it does not convey any intellectually discernable message. We do not know what Humpty Dumpty is—a personified egg-man, a short squat man, a pure figment of imagination, or, as some say, a cannon—nor do we know why Humpty had a great fall—was it an accident, a suicide, or did someone perhaps dump him off the wall? Regardless, we sympathize when we hear that poor Humpty experienced such a great fall that not even all of the king's horses and men could put him together again.

A pattern that connects produces meaningfulness by creating a sense of affinity, or by conveying a message. If Sisyphus was rolling rocks to the top of a hill to build something resembling a house there, we would easily discern the meaning of his activity. With Humpty Dumpty, our positive reaction is based on affinity and not on any message we can discern. When we feel or intuit that sense of affinity, we respond to it not just with our minds but with our entire organism. Like movements in a dance, the words of this nursery rhyme create a sense of rhythmic pulsation, which is a fundamental characteristic of all life. Everything that is meaningful seems to presuppose something of that kind: it either resembles the rhythmic pulsation of life or serves those pulsations that enable life to maintain or enhance itself.

The effect of the rhythm is not due to merely perceiving a pattern outside us but to our becoming patterned ourselves. When we hear a song we like, we began to hum along, or even to adjust the movements of our entire body to follow the beat of the song. We can thus say that we experience as meaningful those happenings in which we recognize a certain measure and that as a result of our affinity to the measure, we ourselves become measured and behave in a measured way.

It seems, then, that the meaning of life boils down to two elements that need to complement each other. First, there is life, with all its pulsations and functions, the meaning of which we are investigating. Second, there is a measured pattern of living. The words measure and measured usually suggest something quantitative, but this is not what we are concerned about here. To avoid this connotation, let us try using the language of norms and normativity, in place of that of measures and measurement. Norms and normativity indicate qualitative and value-based standards of life. Life itself is neither the highest value nor inherently meaningful. A meaningful life seems to be possible when one lives in accordance with certain norms, which in themselves are not arbitrary but integrally connected with life and lead to its flourishing.

Moral norms are the first that come to mind when we think about the meaning of life. They deal with what is good and evil, right and wrong. In his well-known book, *Mere Christianity*, C. S. Lewis called the distinction between right and wrong a clue to the meaning of the universe. He also maintained that the moral principles of fair play and decent behavior belong to the very infrastructure of the world: they hold it together and establish a frame within which life can be meaningful. Moreover, they instruct us that the things that happen to us are based on merit, on what we deserve. We do not know why Humpty Dumpty had a great fall, but we do know why Sisyphus had to roll the rock uphill: he was punished by the gods for being deceitful and murdering his guests, thereby violating one of the oldest and most sacred of the ancient moral norms: the law of hospitality. Sisyphus got what he deserved. According to Lewis' understanding, morality is of central importance for a meaningful life: the meaning of life is structured around measure and normativity, and merit seems to be precisely the pattern that connects the various aspects of life into a meaningful whole.

Merit and the Value of Human Life

Natural death is as much a part of the rhythmic order of the universe as birth. Such death is a part of the nonviolent order of the cosmos, but death due to murder is not. This may be the reason why, almost universally, murder is considered to be a mortal sin against life, regardless of what value life may have.

Nevertheless, respect for a human life is not the highest moral value: it is not in the rank of values like friendship and love, faith and trustworthiness. A magnificent artistic exploration of the complexities involved in this issue is presented by Fyodor Dostoevsky in his novel *Crime and Punishment*. The title itself points to the principle of merit, and the content of the novel reveals further subtleties associated with this principle. A poor and hungry student, Raskolnikov, kills an old woman, a greedy and merciless pawnbroker, to take her money. He despises her for squeezing the last valuables out of desperate people like himself, but upon learning that she wants to donate all her money to an already wealthy monastery after her death, he is "prompted" to act. (He also wants to prove that he can be like Napoleon and step over dead bodies, but of that later.)

Raskolnikov does not want any of her money for himself; he believes that it is only proper to use that money to help those who are even poorer than he is. Despite his meticulous planning, in the act of execution, things get complicated in a way Raskolnikov did not predict, and his emotions are stirred more than he anticipated: the sister of the old woman returns earlier than expected, and he "has to" kill her as well. Then, some visitors are knocking at the door of the old lady's apartment, and he barely manages to escape without being seen.

Raskolnikov runs away from the apartment without finding most of the money, the supposed motive for the murder. From a utilitarian point of view, which guided Raskolnikov in planning and executing his action, the life of the old pawnbroker may have been useless and nothing but an obstacle to the money being used for humane purposes. After the murder, Raskolnikov realizes that his utilitarian calculus was profoundly misguided. A line that should not have been crossed was breached by his act, and punishment had to follow. Dostoevsky masterfully described how that penance took the form of mental torture that was greater than any physical punishment for such a crime normally is.

This story reinforces our fundamental conviction that every human life is valuable. This is the case regardless of positive individual qualities, or a lack thereof. Together with many Christians, Dostoevsky was prone to believe this because of his religious orientation. But such a judgment can be accepted without invoking any religious view. It can made on moral grounds. For example, Schweitzer defended an ethical approach known as "reverence for life," which he defined as follows: it is good to maintain and enhance life; it is bad to destroy life or to obstruct it. Schweitzer meant that we should value and respect every life, including nonhuman life. He did not mean to overvalue life by proclaiming it as the highest good. As a medical doctor, virtually every day he was in the position to destroy many lives (of dangerous microorganisms, for example) to preserve the lives of his human patients and heal them. Schweitzer's view was chiefly aimed against our habitual underestimation of the value of life: as the history of humankind demonstrates, without any good reason for doing so we kill all too easily—not only other living beings but humans as well.

Schweitzer's definition of good and evil does not deal only with killing versus maintaining life but also with enhancing versus obstructing life. We need to accept that life is not created by human beings and that even our own lives are not our possessions to do with as we want. Rather, they are entrusted to our care. They are our foundations on which something greater than sheer life can and should be built. What, exactly? Schweitzer spoke about developing our gifts and flourishing as humans, which he understood as raising our natural relationship to the world to a moral and a broadly understood spiritual level. This was Schweitzer's way of explaining in what a meaningful life consists.

Like Dostoevsky and C. S. Lewis, Schweitzer was convinced of the interpenetration of the natural and moral aspects of life, with regard to both any individual life and the cosmos as a whole. The order that governs our lives and the pulsation of the entire cosmos seems to be not only synchronized but also morally oriented. We do not understand many happenings in the world, but the order that pervades them all seems to have the mechanism of deserving and fulfillment built in. The relationship of causes and effects occurring in the world seems to include the concept of fairness, or in a broad sense, justice. The recorded proverbs of various cultures and epochs capture this belief. In the Orient, the proverb says that every work bears its fruit. In the biblical tradition, we say that we reap what we sow. In the secular context, we speak about getting what we deserve.

Few principles are as deeply ingrained as that of merit; our lives would hardly make sense without keeping it in mind. We raise our children by trying to make them adhere to it as something as fundamental as $2 + 2 = 4$. We teach them that whatever they want to get or accomplish, from the smallest things to the greatest, they have to earn them. By teaching children that fulfillment can only follow deserving, we help them to integrate into wider social networks and to function within them successfully. The same approach is valid for adults: whatever we want to accomplish in life, we need to be reasonable, restrained, and work hard for it. Sooner or later, patience and dedication will pay off. And when they do, it is easy to see that we would perceive life as meaningful. The foundation for its meaning is laid down in the very nature of the universe. It is up to us, then, up to our efforts and actions, whether our lives will be meaningful—and to what degree.

Merit, Karma, and the Golden Rule

There are multiple ways in which the principle of merit is further interpreted. The most elaborate of them is through the Hindu doctrine of *karma*. This doctrine is a combination of complex metaphysical, physical, and moral views: it involves belief in the reincarnation of the soul, as well as in the essential prearranged relatedness of the world-soul (*Brahman*) with the soul of every individual (*Atman*). Despite its layers of complexity, the core of this doctrine is simple: it teaches of a universal bondage tying together everything that exists in one tightly connected system of causes and effects. The doctrine of karma presupposes a complete determination according to which no act, however insignificant, happens without causing a ripple effect on the future. Since Hindus believe that we live many lives in different forms and reincarnations, karma regulates not only what occurs in the present but also what will happen in our future lives.

Even someone like Gandhi believed in the power of karma. Yet he understood it with a characteristic twist. Gandhi emphasized that we are responsible for the morality of our thoughts and actions, insofar as they have a causal relation with the past and the future. Since we cannot escape from the karmic chain of causation, and since the use of brute force can only lead to bad blood and desire for revenge, unlike Raskolnikov and the vast majority of people in the world, Gandhi insisted that we should be as nonviolent as possible and treat each other as brothers and sisters. Only in that way, Gandhi believed, can we transform the bad karma into its opposite.

While advocating this view, Gandhi was influenced not only by Hinduism but also by the biblical tradition. In the Old Testament, the Ten Commandments issued by God and delivered to the Hebrews by Moses specify the most important prohibitions, the ones that should never be violated. Part of that tradition is also the idea of a covenant between God and (His chosen) people. That covenant includes a promise that, if people follow the word and law of God, He guarantees that they will be preserved and flourish. The New Testament shifts the emphasis toward our contributions to the future salvation of our souls; it urges us to make ourselves worthy of the coming of the Kingdom of God.

The biblical tradition includes several references to what is widely known as the Golden Rule. In its negative formulation, it warns us not to behave toward others in ways that we would not like to be treated by them. In the positive conveyance, the Rule urges us to behave toward other human beings as we would like to be treated by them. Together with "Do not kill," the Golden Rule is probably the most universally accepted moral precept in the world. It is hard to know its origin with any definitiveness, but we usually take it to have been formulated for the first time by Confucius, or within the Confucian school of thought, of which Mencius was a successor.

Neither the principle of merit nor the Golden Rule require any divine legitimization. This is what gives them even wider appeal. In the secular context, the principle of merit is presented through the concept of justice. Understood roughly as fairness, this concept is treated as moral, rather than as divinely implemented. The idea of justice is so fundamental not only because it draws a line between right and wrong but because it also curbs our crude egoism: if we are to live in one community, not everything can be for ourselves. We should live by the same standards that apply to us all. The ideal of equality is basic to such a concept of justice: we must have equal rights and duties; we must all be subject to the same socially accepted laws. Then, we can gather in a circle as one community and attempt to live as meaningfully as possible.

Challenging the Principle of Merit

It is understandable why the principle of merit has such universal appeal and why human lives have to be morally sound to be considered meaningful. There must be something right about it: some decency that is respected and some line that is upheld; some good that is earned and some goal that is fulfilled. Nevertheless, the principle of merit has also been accompanied by persistent doubts. As much as justice is important, it is only one of the fundamental moral values. In fact, it is the most elementary and lowest among them—a foundation on which other moral values may be pursued. For human life to be meaningful in any robust sense, a whole spectrum of other values may be required. Christians insist on brotherly love, and most of us desire happiness and personal love. Let us also not forget about nonmoral values—like the values of aesthetic appreciation and creativity, humor and playfulness—which also seem indispensable to leading a meaningful life. Some of these other values may have little to do with justice or may even stand in opposition to it, yet they appear unquestionably relevant for a meaningful life. If this is so, then the principle of merit is far from being sufficient to account for how our lives become meaningful.

Applying justice often involves more complex issues than the principle of merit indicates. After the trial of Socrates, for example, Plato wondered which is worse: To do wrong or to suffer wrong? Socrates did not seem to do anything wrong, yet he was accused by his contemporaries of corrupting the youth and not believing in the gods that were officially celebrated. He was found guilty and sentenced to death. Although convinced that he was innocent, Socrates accepted the death sentence and rejected the proposal of his friend Crito to organize his escape from jail. One wrong, insisted Socrates, cannot be corrected by committing another one.

Most of us think that it is preferrable to do wrong than to suffer wrong. We believe, for example, that it is wrong to kill other human beings, but when our own existence is threatened by the aggressive actions of others, killing others in self-defense may be justified, especially if done as a last resort. Plato's Socrates categorically asserted that it is better to suffer wrong than to do wrong, even in the case of self-defense. This view has been key to many defenders of nonviolence and nonviolent resistance, from Mahavira, Buddha, and Jesus to Tolstoy, Gandhi, and King.

In his most celebrated dialogue, *Republic*, Plato argued that the person who suffers wrong may still be 729 times happier than the person who does wrong. How Plato got this exact number and whether this is indeed the right ratio does not matter. Plato's point is that to enjoy justice is good, but no more than that; to actively practice justice and be just are of a significantly higher value, at least insofar as they pave the way for values of an even higher kind. What Socrates demonstrated during his trial and while awaiting his execution was the value by which he lived his entire life: that of moral dignity. A truly meaningful life is not one in which we do not suffer wrong but one in which we actively strive toward justice.

The most fundamental objection to the principle of merit is that it is simply not part of objective reality, that in reality, the natural and moral elements are not as entwined as the principle of merit presupposes.

From the time of the writing of the ancient Hindu hymns of Rigveda to our age, people have been prone to believing that the universe is on the side of justice. We may like to believe that as well, but is such a claim true?

Since the sixteenth century, Western science has decisively separated the natural and moral aspects of reality: there is no pre-established harmony between deserving and reward. The early modern scientists believed in God but not in an anthropomorphic divinity created in the image of man. Nor did they believe in a world made according to human values: in their view, values are not part of the physical world, nor is the world created with any purpose or design. The events in the world go on, but they do not go anywhere in particular. Like the rock of Sisyphus, which tumbles down every time it is lifted up, the events of the world are governed by laws of nature that have nothing to do with justice and fairness, nor with the designs and desires of human beings. Soon after Newton, even the existence of God was rejected by many scientists as an unnecessary hypothesis. The result was belief in a world in which there is no need for anything holy or sacred. Planet Earth is just a tiny and temporary object in the infinity of being, and man an irrelevant speck of dust in that infinity. For all we know, this desacralized and infinite universe has no center, nor does it need any. Nor can this infinite universe be trusted, for there is nothing to trust—except the mechanical laws of nature. The world is not made for man, nor is any meaning inherent in it. Just as the map of reality should never be confused with the terrain it is supposed to represent, the facts of nature should not be misconceived as revealing any meaning. For any meaning to be possible, man has to adjust to the world as well as he can. If the principle of merit has any significance, it is not as an objective principle incorporated into the real world.

Clearly, the principle of merit is a social principle of the first order. It is incorporated into our legal system, and it is not easy to find any aspect of our social lives in which we treat this principle as irrelevant. Thus, the problem we face is the following. While we expect that the principle of merit has objective and universal validity, social principles are normally nothing more than human conventions, which vary from one society to another and change from one era to another. If the principle of merit is subject to shifts and relativizations, the value that we attach to it is significantly diminished.

There are two lines of thought that attempt to justify the objective validity of this principle and its vital role in our lives' meaning. One of them was outlined by Immanuel Kant, the other by Nicolai Hartmann. Admiring how Newton developed a theory of nature with mathematical precision, Kant thought that we should apply a similar approach to the principles of morality. We would then treat morality not as something that is built into the structure of the real world but as a set of objectively valid principles based on universally applicable laws of reason. Kant was convinced that our rational capacity is governed by the same principles, regardless of our nationality, age, sex, religious affiliation, or social status. Human beings are rational beings, and we should behave in accordance with rationally defensible principles. Such principles are, indeed, subjective insofar as they were created by human beings. But they are also objective and universally binding because they are legitimized by universally valid reason.

Kant defended the law of morality as a categorical imperative. In one of its formulations, it prescribes that we treat other human beings as ends in themselves and never as means only. Just as we can all grasp that $2 + 2 = 4$, or that the law of gravitation implies that every physical body thrown into the air will be pulled down by the gravity of the earth, so we understand that, as rational and moral agents, human beings have absolute value. It is therefore our highest obligation to treat every human being equally, with fairness and respect.

Kant's ethical theory has itself been treated with much respect, but its foundations turned out not to be as secure as he thought. Just as, besides Euclidean geometry, there are alternative forms of geometry, and besides Newtonian physics, there is Einstein's general and special theory of relativity, so the human mind is not as uniform as Kant thought; it need not operate based on one universally shared and unchanging "matrix." Furthermore, what computers are capable of doing in terms of various intellectual operations by far surpasses the possibility of human rationality, yet their algorithmic programming has hardly anything in common with the operating principles of human reason. In the case of human beings, besides reason, our self-interest, as well as our emotions and inclinations, intuitions and moral visions, seem to be as important as Kant's artificially isolated and overly glorified rational capacity—sometimes even more so.

Kant's specific solution cannot be deemed successful. Nevertheless, he did us a great service by calling our attention to the heart of the problem with the principle of merit and its significance for the meaning of life. The key lies in the relationship between what can be called the real and ideal worlds. In an ideal world, virtue is followed by happiness. But we live in the real world, in which virtue is not always appropriately rewarded, nor is it necessarily followed by happiness. Kant recognized the gap between the real and the ideal but thought that it was surmountable. Our principles of reason lead us to keep closing the gap between the two in this life, and our faith will have us believe that the gap will be fully closed in another, heavenly life.

The philosophers who came after Kant rejected his idealism and continued pursing the line of thinking of scientists: the real world should be favored over the ideal world, sheer life over normativity. This is the only realistic approach to life. The whole spectrum of idealism, from Plato to Kant, is untenable. As much as idealism tends toward optimism, a realist orientation leads to pessimism concerning the principle of merit and indirectly to pessimism concerning the possibility of a meaningful life. Schopenhauer developed this line of thinking in his theory of the will that wants to live in accordance with its own urges and desires, not by following any norm imposed from the outside; life cannot have any meaning and purpose beyond itself. Nietzsche followed Schopenhauer's focus on life and reasoned that external norms have no meaning by themselves. Nor are there any promises or contracts in the natural world; they exist only in the social world, as social constructs and as part of social bargains. Like Dostoevsky's Raskolnikov, Nietzsche complained that morality negates life and argued that the meaning of life can consist only in becoming more alive—as alive as we can be.

The existentialist thinkers interpreted Nietzsche's philosophical orientation to imply that there should be no external and normative guidelines to life. We should not try to become what we are supposedly "meant to be," since we are not meant to be anything in particular. We can be whatever we want to be, whatever we choose to be, detached from any externally imposed boundary. Life is just a flow driven by its own internal force, and existence comes before any alleged essence. Existentialists abandon both idealism and realism. The bottom line, in their view, is that there is only an ego: my own self, free-floating and unattached to any anchor. The world has no center and no periphery. Feeling like strangers in the world and excluded from it, existentialists maintain that we are thrown back on ourselves to cope as best we can with our lives and our meaningless universe.

Before we all too conveniently give up on the possibility of an optimistic outlook on life, I would like to outline Hartmann's approach to the relationship between the real and ideal worlds. Hartmann agreed with modern scientists that there is no pre-established harmony between nature and morality, nor between the real and ideal worlds. Nevertheless, he did not go in the direction of vitalism and existentialism, especially with regard to abandoning a view on the essence of human nature and the possibility of a meaningful life entrenched in the nature of being. There is a structure in both the real and ideal worlds, but their structures must be matched differently than we thought previously. Hartmann's leading idea was that the world is built from the bottom up but is made meaningful from the top down. His philosophy has been strangely neglected among contemporary intellectuals. I nevertheless believe that it offers us the most promising approach to the problem of the legitimacy of the principle of merit and its relevance for the possibility of a meaningful life.

Hartmann began his philosophical enterprise by turning toward the real world. He argued that in it we can recognize four layers: the inorganic, the organic, the psychic, and the spiritual. The inorganic world is at the bottom of the "pyramid" of the real. The organic relies on it but introduces a new qualitative phenomenon: life. The psychic depends on the two lower layers for its support, but its qualitative novelty is consciousness, which we do not find in all forms of life. Finally, on top of the layer of psychic being, we can recognize one more stratum—that of the spiritual. The spirit does not descend from above, as the Christian tradition postulates, but emerges from below. For us human beings, the spirit is the highest known layer in the pyramid of the real world. We recognize the spiritual realm of reality through its three main manifestations: as individual personalities (subjective spirit), as collective phenomena such as art, science, and language (objective spirit), and as institutions, in the form of schools, museums, concert halls, churches, or courthouses (objectified spirit).

Hartmann's central insight was that in any hierarchy the highest layer is actually the weakest, while the lowest layers are the strongest. Those beings which exist in the highest layer must embody the elements of the lower layers but not the other way around. Personality is not possible without consciousness, a living body, and inorganic matter, but what is merely inorganic matter need not be alive, conscious, or spiritual. Regardless of the layers to which they belong, all real beings, without exception, are concrete individuals that have a temporal although not necessarily a spatial dimension: our thoughts and desires, memories and feelings, occur in time but not in space.

Hartmann maintained that there are two mutually irreducible but deeply interrelated modes of being: the real and the ideal. By ideal being, he did not mean fantasies or arbitrary thoughts in the minds of people, or rational ideas in the Kantian universal reason, or ideals in the mind of God, or perfect Platonic Forms. Hartmann's conception of ideal being was closest to that of Plato, yet different from it in some significant elements. Mathematical ideas and principles may be the clearest examples of ideal beings. The validity of the Pythagorean theorem does not depend on the existence of any triangle in the real world, the sum of whose internal angles would add up to exactly 180 degrees. Mathematical ideas have their own internal necessity that does not depend on what exists in the real world. They are such, however, that at least under some favorable circumstances, they can be realized in the real world. Expressed more generally, while ideal being does not in any way depend on the real, real being is so structured that it allows the actualization of the ideal in the real being. This view misled Plato to believe that the world of ideal Forms is also the only true reality, while what we usually consider real is only images and shadows on the walls of the proverbial cave.

According to Hartmann, Plato made a significant "category" mistake. He mixed up the categories that belong to the real and the ideal worlds. The concrete beings that we experience in our daily lives are, indeed, imperfect and transitory, unlike the unchanging and universally valid principles of the ideal world. This recognition does not imply, however, that what is concrete and transitory is not real; in fact, there is no other kind of reality but the concrete and transitory one. General and universally valid ideas and ideals need never be realized in the real world, but they are and remain examples of ideal beings that have universal and objective validity.

Hartmann's view of the relationship of real and ideal being is especially relevant for our discussion of the principle of merit and the meaning of life when we focus on values. Values are intimately connected with meaning: meaning is not about facts but about something that matters, that has value that we estimate and pursue. The principle of merit sums it all up by urging us to pursue what is valuable—as valuable as possible—as a path toward a meaningful life.

The issue of the origin and validity of values has always posed serious problems. Religious views, such as those of Christianity, offer an elegant solution: God is the author of everything, including values, and He creates the world from dust by imposing certain patterns and values on it. The issues of the author and the authorization of values are thus solved in one move because they come from the same source. When we start sharply separating facts and values—or the "is" and the "ought," as philosophers call them—and argue that no "ought" can be derived from any "is" —both where values come from and how their validity can be objective become very problematic. If Kant's universal reason is not the source of values, and neither imposes nor guarantees the validity of values, then it seems the only paths open are those of conventionalism and instrumentalism, or subjectivism and relativism.

Hartmann's conception of real and ideal being enabled him to pursue a quite different and far more promising path. He maintained that, like mathematical ideas, values are also ideal beings. This means that, as we do not create such mathematical ideas and yet assume their validity to be objective, we can treat values in a similar manner. We do not invent values, whether they are moral, aesthetic, cognitive, or vital. Just as good is always valuable, so is beauty, so is truth, and so is health. We do not make such values, nor do we confer validity on them. Fairness and truthfulness are valuable and should be valued even if there is no actual society in which they are fully appreciated and in which corruption and money are not what make society function. Similarly, truth is truth, beauty is beauty, and they have their own uncontestable values, regardless of whether we live in accordance with them or even recognize them for what they are in the first place.

Hartmann on Two Scales of Moral Values

Nicolai Hartmann (1882-1950) believed that contemporary philosophers rejected the idea that there are objective and absolute values because we cannot establish one unified and infallible scale of moral values. Hartmann maintained that these two are separable issues. There can be objective and absolute values, although we use two irreducible scales of moral values. We rely on two scales because there is a genuine plurality of values, which makes them irreducible to any one value, and because values display different dimensions: height and strength. Some values, such as friendship and trust, purity and nobility, are high. Other moral values, such as justice and solidarity, self-control and modesty, are low. Interestingly, lower values are usually very strong: they are stable. By contrast, higher values tend to be weak: they are unstable and not necessary for the maintenance of life itself. The lower values are foundational for human life, while the higher and weaker values are not. Hartmann connected the meaning of life with the pursuit and realization of higher values: realizing them is exalting, liberating, and inspiring. Nevertheless, he emphasized that the lower values are as indispensable for the moral life as the highest values. Our moral life is perverted if it relates only to the highest values while neglecting the lower values, as though it were possible to actualize the former, suspended in space without a foundation in the latter.

The principle of merit is not built into the structure of the real world. Neither is it a mere fiction, nor a convenient instrumental educational tool. The principle of merit is part of the ideal world, and has the same validity as do the principles of mathematics and other ideal values. Like everything else that resides in the ideal world, the principle of merit need not be applied to the real world. But it could be. We can choose to live in accordance with it, and we can decide to bring as much justice and kindness, beauty and health as possible into the world. Like Plato's Forms and Kant's categorical imperative, the principle of merit shines above the world and could be our guide through the turbulent waters of life. And just as Kant realized that even if we live in accordance with the categorical imperative, virtue does not guarantee happiness, living in accordance with the principle of merit does not guarantee a meaningful life. This is so not because the principle of merit is irrelevant for the meaning of life, but rather because it is not the only factor that matters and determines whether and to what extent our lives are meaningful. Our determination to be as fair and honest, as caring and loving persons as we can is indeed of great importance in our attempts to live meaningful lives. But external circumstances, which may bring us good luck or bad luck, are also factors that should not be overlooked.

Chapter 2
Luck

Life as a Gamble

When we travel to previously unknown places, we are always surprised by how people live. We listen to their stories and learn their customs and sometimes wonder whether we would want to be like them, living where and how they do, or the opposite. We use a variety of phrases to articulate these impressions, but they point toward two phenomena: good luck and bad luck. Some people have the good luck to be born in a prosperous family or at a place where we can only dream of living. Others seem to get one bad break after another. Does not luck—both good luck and bad luck—have a significant impact on the meaning of life?

A preliminary answer to this question is that luck can definitely have an impact on the meaning of life. And it also seems justified to say that luck, like merit, need not be the only factor that determines the meaning of our lives. When we think of this further, it appears that with respect to luck, there is an asymmetry that is not present in the case of merit: no matter how great good luck is, it can never guarantee that its beneficiary will lead a good and meaningful life; bad luck, by contrast, can be so devastating that it may preclude the very possibility of a meaningful life. Our luck can be so bad as to lead us to give up on our lives, or to eventually hide behind self-imposed delusions, in order to gather enough strength to continue our miserable experience.

Let us deepen our understanding of both merit and luck by first traveling back to our distant past. A remarkable revolution occurred over the course of several centuries before Christ: a spiritual revolution. In various areas around the globe, stretching from China and India to Persia, Greece, and all the way to Egypt, seemingly independently of each other, various peoples came to surprisingly similar realizations. They came to believe, not that there is a transcendent divine force—most of them had believed that, in one form or another, for centuries—but that there is an essential correlation between that force and human existence. The central insights, with many local variations, were that human existence contains in itself something resembling that divine force that governs all there is; that both the divine force and the corresponding force in human beings are spiritual, rather than purely physical or material; and that the goal of human life is to attune our existence to the working of that divine force. Since that time, some have thought that the core of the universe and its central moving force are spiritual, and since human beings are also endowed with spirit, the goal of our lives should be to develop our spiritual capacity and, through its guidance, achieve harmony with that greater spiritual force. As Joseph Campbell poetically expressed it, the goal of life is to make our heartbeat match the beat of the universe, to match our nature with Nature.

The "philosophy" that promoted these insights was eventually labeled "perennial" because these thoughts were supposed to capture the unchanging Truths. Karl Jaspers called this period, stretching from roughly the eighth to the third century before Christ, the "Axial Age" because it established a cluster of beliefs around which human beings centered their understanding of the world, of themselves, and of their place and role in reality. The principle of merit was one of the expressions of that spiritual revolution.

The world, according to this perennial philosophy, is not only well-ordered but also two-layered: it is the intercrossing of the sacred and the profane. This world is measured and proportioned, good and beautiful.

Despite the vastness of the cosmos, human beings have a secure place and an important role in it—if we could only learn to live in these two domains at once. We want to be at home in this world and for our lives to be mirror images of the pre-established harmony. Although we can only control our efforts, and not their outcomes, we have every reason to hope that in such a harmonious world, the deserving would be granted fulfillment, good would prevail over evil, and a virtuous life would be meaningful.

> ### Eliade on the Sacred and the Profane
>
> The religious historian Mircea Eliade (1907-1986) examined a distinction between the profane and the sacred. He understood them as two separable but interacting modes of existence. The profane is what is ordinary and what we manipulate in our practical endeavors. The sacred is what is so precious that it should never be compromised or violated. The central function of the sacred is to make our orientation possible; it reveals to us what needs to be valued beyond–and sometimes despite–ordinary things and values. Eliade reminded us that one and the same thing can be treated as both profane and sacred. A rock, for example, on which Abraham was to sacrifice Isaak, can be seen as nothing but a rock, but it can also be seen as something else: a holy place and axis mundi– the spiritual center of the world. For a nonreligious individual who denies the existence of the sacred, the

> universe is opaque and homogeneous, inert and mute; it transmits no message and holds no cipher. Eliade argued that this does not mean, however, that such an individual is without religion altogether. Our choice does not seem to be about being religious. Rather, it is about whether we are going to worship a god or an idol. Consciously or unconsciously, the vast majority of human beings still hold to various religious and mythological concepts and residues. Religion and mythology present messages to us symbolically. When taken seriously, insisted Eliade, such symbols and messages not only "open" the world for us but also enable us to connect our particularities and uniqueness with universal and everlasting values and ideals. In that way, symbols intertwine our profane individual experiences with the sacred. That is how we can connect the real and the ideal and live in accordance with what is most sacred to us.

This is a marvelous view to adhere to: it is idealistic and reassuring, optimistic and uplifting. Unfortunately, our life experience is often incongruent with it. Many people enjoy the benefits of life without deserving them in any way. These individuals need not be evil persons, but neither are they particularly virtuous; nevertheless, fortune smiles on them in a variety of ways, or over longer periods. That does not necessarily mean that every aspect of their lives is "milk and honey," but they do seem to have an unfair advantage over the rest of us—whether it consists of a particularly supportive family and happy childhood, extraordinary health and other gifts of nature, extremely favorable material or spiritual conditions of life, or an energizing job and stimulating work environment. The fact that they get to be so lucky does not make us admire them, but it is hard not to envy those who find themselves in such circumstances. Life is a series of ordeals, and there is a long journey in front of each of us to achieve what can be properly called a meaningful life. Yet, people who seem to be born under a lucky star either begin their lives' journey from a more favorable starting position than the rest of us, or get an occasional lift along the way.

What should we say, however, about those whose bad luck never seems to end? Or those who experience such devastating losses that they can hardly recover? What consolation could they have for being decent, honest, hardworking persons? What order and measure, goodness and beauty, can they experience in a life that persistently abuses them just because they happen to be born in a certain religious or social group or are of a particular race or sex? What can people hope for, what can they believe in, when a tragic set of circumstances devastates their families or themselves for no obvious moral or rational reason?

If we have not experienced such things ourselves, we have been in the presence of people who have. And we are well aware that in circumstances in which something is irretrievably lost, or broken beyond repair, all words of consolation and attempts to revive the hope of these people seem empty and pointless.

A realistic approach to life steers us toward pessimism by undermining our hope and disintegrating our trust in the workings of the world. In extreme cases, it leads toward indifference or skepticism: a sense of the malfunctioning or futility of all things. When we start ignoring the sacred aspect of existence, when we forget about the world-soul and the divine force, in harmony with which we are supposed to live, and rely primarily on our own eyes and ears, we see mostly suffering and pain. Typically, such experiences occur in one of two familiar scenarios, both of which undermine the principle of merit: something that should happen according to our reasonable and idealistic expectations does not happen; or what, according to our system of beliefs and morality, should not happen does in fact take place.

There is hardly a generation that has not experienced major wars, pandemics, or natural disasters—or all of them. People die in the hundreds and thousands, sometimes even millions. Many more are left with maimed bodies, broken homes, and devastated lands. Millions feel forced to leave their destroyed homes and migrate, hoping for a better future, only to realize that no other land will welcome them and that their presence sparks hostility, even violence, toward them. Their misfortunes are multiplied, not eliminated. The two chief lessons of human history seem to be that it is much easier to obstruct and destroy than to build and grow, and that, in order to get what they want, human beings rarely restrain themselves from using the most destructive force that they have at their disposal—even against innocent bystanders.

When we face the world with open eyes and ears, it is hard to "praise the Lord" for His majestic creation. When we are realists, it feels more accurate to repeat the claim of one of Shakespeare's characters that the world is a tale told by an idiot. Realism provokes doubt and skepticism and, only a few decades after Shakespeare, René Descartes entertained the possibility that, if there is a divine being, it is an "evil demon." Such a being does not take human beings as partners in maintaining and governing the world; instead, he makes fun of us and uses us as toys for his evil schemes and perverted entertainment. And if there is no such devious god, we may be better off inventing one, for how else do we make sense of this senseless world?

We live in an age when it is far easier to believe that evil prevails over good and that we are strangers in this world, than to believe that we are living in a welcoming home. Similar to the COVID-19 pandemic that is spreading across the globe, so much in our world appears random and contingent, senseless and meaningless. Something in us, however, rebels against accepting such a view. Just as our bodies need structure and order, our souls need something to believe in. We yearn for a spiritual home as much as we yearn to make sense of what is happening around us. To satisfy those urges, we are willing to invent all sorts of "explanations," however unsupported by facts or irrational they may be, rather than accept what is happening as completely random.

When things "do not make sense," it seems easier to blame "destiny" and some deity—like Fortuna—than to accept that we are clueless. In ancient Rome, the goddess Fortuna symbolized the capricious force that seems to control human life. Fortuna was considered inexorable: not malevolent but simply indifferent to the consequences of her whims. This is why she was depicted with a rudder: she was the deity who was supposed to be steering us through the waters of life. The problem was that Fortuna was also depicted as blind since she did not know where she was taking her followers. Life is an adventure, the Romans believed, with an unpredictable outcome. This is why they held that no life can be rightly pronounced meaningful while it lasts. Such a judgment can be made after human beings reach their final destination, and the whole journey of their lives becomes clearly visible. Life is a gamble; only at its end can we decide whether it was ultimately a success or a failure.

Luck versus Utility

Reasonable and educated persons know that one should not be tricked by explanations and accusations based on ignorance and superstition. Our beliefs and judgments should be supported by evidence and based on sound reasoning. For at least the last five centuries, since natural science separated the profane from the sacred, facts from values, and mechanical from anthropomorphic explanations, we have been taught to believe that we live in a world without purpose and without a goal. We live in a world of random occurrences, which by itself can hardly be meaningful.

This rationally reconstructed world is no less confusing than the one it is supposed to replace. The ultimate reality, we are now told, consists not of the invisible God but of invisible particles. Our senses do not see any particles. Science tells us that up to seventy percent of our bodies is made of water. When we look at other human beings or at ourselves in the mirror, we see solid bodies, and all our choices and behaviors are predicated on our belief that human beings are indeed solid entities. Can we, for instance, blame particles and water for being mean to us? And if not, how do we live in this confusing world?

To understand this better, let us reconsider a few more implications of the scientific revolution, insofar as they were directed against the views of the perennial philosophy. The elimination of the world-soul and the focus on the world-body of modern science, together with its separation of ontology and ethics, shifts the emphasis from the spiritual to the material aspects of life and undermines the principle of merit. This principle presupposes that there are values that are stable and absolute. With the end of the Middle Ages and the beginning of the modern era, our understanding of values undergoes a radical transformation. Instead of stable and absolute values sanctioned by God, or at least values that are inherent in the nature of things, we are left on our own.

At that intersection, one omnipresent but otherwise marginal criterion of values assumed a central role: utility. If there is no world-soul, but only the soul of man, we should not worry about how to adjust to the divine force and attune to its values. It is not God who is the "measure of all things" but our collective or individual humanity. Instead of us serving as vehicles for a higher force, the soul-less and value-less world should serve us—or at least be used by us as the raw material for satisfying our needs.

Utility is a relative value. There is no utility *per se*, but only usefulness for this purpose or that person, even if the same thing is of no use for another person or purpose. This kind of approach to values is what encouraged Raskolnikov to think of murdering the old pawnbroker. If there are no absolute values, there can be no absolute prohibitions either. The Ten Commandments and the principle of merit should be archived on the dusty shelves of human history. Despite the unconditional commandment not to kill, we have always recognized the right to kill in self-defense. What is more, in the natural world, killing occurs all the time: life lives on life. Since reality is so detached from ideality and traditionally understood morality, why not murder if the beneficial consequences significantly outweigh the loss of a life that is more or less worthless? There is no particular reason why one individual would happen to be more valuable than any other. It is just a random fact that it is so, sheer luck. At another time or place, or for another person, it could just as easily be the other way around.

The rejection of divinity and focus on utility go hand in hand with the shift of attention to measurable things and tangible values. Together with a possessive attitude toward the world, the relationship of means and ends becomes crucial in our attitudes toward each other. Instead of religion and spirituality, politics and economy become dominant in people's lives. While hailed as realistic, the dominance of politics and economy represents a triumph of fiction over reality—a fiction based on ambition and greed, possessiveness and exploitation.

Means and Ends

The principle of merit can also be presented in terms of means and ends. Morally appropriate behavior is then seen as the means for the achievement of the desired end: a virtuous and meaningful life. Seen from this perspective, one significant problem with the principle of merit is that we can control the means but not the end. We can keep our part of the bargain, but when the desired outcome is not realized—or when, due to bad luck, the opposite of the desired outcome occurs—whom should we blame? And if our efforts are continuously frustrated, should we not question whether there is such a bargain in the first place?

When we stop believing that there is a hidden but securely centered moral and rational order to the world, we almost spontaneously shift our attention from means to ends. Instead of the principle of merit, we accept the principle that the ends justify the means. We want the outcome, regardless of how we get it. If the important end is to be wealthy, for instance, then it does not matter whether it is accomplished by means of "old" money or "new" money, in the accepted and legal ways, or in ways that are not so. Or so it seems. F. Scott Fitzgerald explored this topic beautifully in his novel, *The Great Gatsby*. In the US of the 1920s, getting rich was treated as the eleventh commandment. Any attempt to make a clear-cut differentiation between right and wrong ways to get rich appeared irrelevant. Without an underlying harmony between the divine and the human, and without the traditional morality that separates right and wrong, it all becomes an improvisation, it all becomes "jazz." With his money, Jay Gatsby throws the wildest, most fabulous parties in town. He becomes the latest wonder in a glittering and forever fluctuating world. The ball is on, the music is blasting, the dancers are swirling, but what happens when the party ends? Or even more importantly for Gatsby, when Daisy—the only person for whom he cares and for whom he wants to be wealthy—does not show up? Well, what else but—spend more money! With so much money to throw around, there must be a way to get what we want. Is there anything—or anyone—that money cannot buy if we make the bid high enough?

If getting wealthy is the eleventh commandment, then we also need a twelfth commandment, and a few more as well. (Martin Luther King, Jr., wittily pointed out one of them: Do not get caught!) Getting wealthy can allow many miracles to happen, but none of them can be an end in itself. When his wealth and cunning finally enable Gatsby to hold Daisy in his arms, a happy ending seems imminent. But life is random and Daisy soon slips away again, carried by the ever-swirling jazz of life. Due to both unpredictable complications in the plot and bad luck, Gatsby is killed. The music at his mansion comes to a stop, while the enormous crowd that used to attend his magnificent parties moves to another place where the music—as loud and dazzling as ever—continues. At Gatsby's funeral, only two people show up: his poor neighbor Nick and his long-estranged father, who had quite different aspirations for his gifted son.

The great Jay Gatsby is gone, but the music—always the symbol of life and one of the most accurate reflections of its values—does not stop. Nor does the chain of means and ends ever end. Getting rich looks like an end, but an end for what? And is there an end for anything as shifting as the fortunes of life? What seems to be an end in one case becomes a means for another end. And throughout that process, as in Gatsby's story, the chain of means and ends becomes more and more estranged from the reality of life, which has to come to a stop at some point. Then, a judgment on life's meaning can finally be pronounced.

Luck versus Happiness

In her magisterial book, *The Human Condition*, Hannah Arendt demonstrated that there is a significant dissimilarity between utility and meaningfulness. The disparity between the two is reflected in the linguistic gap between "in order to" and "for the sake of." "For the sake of" indicates a definitive end, and insofar as it pertains to meaning, meaning itself must be something stable, perhaps even permanent. Yet, in the surface-oriented and one-dimensional world of usefulness, there can be nothing permanent. When usefulness is made the ultimate criterion of value, with utility as its goal, it defeats its own purpose. When "in order to" gets confused with "for the sake of" and utility gets mistaken as meaning, utility can only generate meaninglessness, not meaning.

What, then, is the relationship among luck, happiness, and a meaningful life? People pray to the goddess Fortuna for three things: fertility, prosperity, and victory. What else is there in life to wish for? While children are unquestionably an enormous responsibility, they are also an immense source of joy and pride, and they can continue the legacy of their parents. That legacy consists mostly of prosperity. When there is prosperity, it becomes easier to have a good and honorable name—or to make it such. And since life is a struggle, in which some battles are more consequential than others, we need to be victorious in at least the most important fights of our lives. Such victories bring more honor, in addition to fame and glory. Where such external circumstances of life are well aligned, we expect that the corresponding positive feelings will be present as well. These feelings can be called the pleasures of life, regardless of whether they refer to the simple joys of life or those special moments of euphoria and exuberance. When the goddess Fortuna is on our side—and as long as she is—life can indeed be prosperous and joyous. Life is then considered happy.

This is a familiar and easily understandable conception of happiness. Those who believe in it realize, however, that the wheel of fortune always turns. Like the sun at its zenith or the full moon, the wheel of fortune revolves. A glorious afternoon gives way to dusk, soon to be followed by darkness, just as the full moon starts slowly disappearing each consecutive night, coming to the point at which it does not appear in the sky for three full nights. These are nothing but the stages in the process; what is down, submerged in the darkness, reappears again in the light. Dragging the flow of life with it, the wheel of fortune continues its endless spin.

In addition to this conception of happiness, which is closely tied to luck, there is another one. To be happy is not to be at the zenith of the wheel of fortune, but rather in the hub of the wheel, in its center. It is understood then that happiness is something rare and elusive, not necessarily characterized by pleasures and favorable circumstances but by harmonious and stable arrangements that are often understood in terms of individual flourishing and fulfillment. Philosophers never tire of emphasizing that this is what the Greek word *eudaimonia* really meant, despite our customary translation of it as happiness. Nevertheless, philosophers cannot find a way to agree among themselves as to what flourishing means or in what it consists.

Be that as it may, we are now discussing happiness as good fortune. Taken in this sense, anyone can be happy, from children to those who are ignorant or uncaring, and even deluded or wicked persons. On one side of this spectrum, happiness is due to innocence not yet hampered by the hardness of life. On the other side, happiness is due to a stroke of luck—winning the lottery, not being caught in a profitable crime, or finding a person who desires us—at least for a while.

Happiness due to good luck cannot be identified with the meaning of life. While it may contribute to life's meaning, it could also be detrimental to it. It would be foolish to deny that it is better to have good luck than bad luck. While possessive attachment to material things can be blinding and misleading, there is nothing particularly virtuous or appealing about poverty and deprivation. Harsh conditions can make it difficult to flourish and lead a virtuous and meaningful life. While the occasional plant finds a way to grow even in an almost impossible position on the side of a cliff, it is easier for a plant to sprout in a well-watered garden with fertile soil and plenty of sunshine. But the opposite phenomenon is also well-known, although we tend to forget about it. Favorable life circumstances could make us unmotivated and sluggish. What is too easily obtained is usually not respected for its worth: easy come, easy go. The sweetness of life is hardly possible to appreciate without tasting the bitter side of life as well.

All this is well-known. What is less frequently understood is what can be called the paradox of happiness: we can bear only a limited measure of happiness without sinking morally. One part of that paradox is due to what appears to be our nature: we cannot sustain exclusive cultivation of one value without causing damage; the extremes have to be balanced by their opposites. In the case of happiness, the paradox consists of the interconnectedness of happiness and its counterpart—suffering. Whether we like it or not, suffering can provide what happiness lacks: the ability to sharpen our perception of values. Like poverty or illness, suffering makes us better appreciate what we have to earn on our own. Any deeper conception of happiness has to account for the possibility of the coexistence of happiness and suffering: just as there can be no life without suffering, there can be no happiness without suffering. It is equally hard to imagine that a life can be meaningful without suffering.

Happiness and Suffering

Our contemporary world is preoccupied with happiness. But it may be suffering, not happiness, that deserves our closer attention—both in the context of the meaning of life and in general. There is much suffering in the world. Some of it is deserved, as the principle of merit stipulates, but more of it appears to be the result of bad luck and unfavorable circumstances. In our developed and civilized Western world, suffering is viewed in an overly negative way. This may be an overreaction to the dominance of the Axial Age when suffering was ascribed an exaggerated spiritual value. For all those who refuse to glorify martyrs and who see the world as black or white, suffering is nothing but a disvalue that should be avoided at all costs.

Such views are, indeed, in stark contrast to those promoted during the Axial Age. The Buddha, for example, saw life as suffering. He did not glorify suffering but stated what he believed to be a fundamental insight about life that our thinking and action must take into consideration. In Buddhism, these insights are further illustrated by bodhisattvas, persons who refuse to exit this life of suffering and enter Nirvana as long as there are human beings still suffering. Suffering-with, or com-passion, is a fundamental human virtue—in Buddhism, Christianity, and, to one degree or another, in every other spiritual tradition. If life is to be affirmed, suffering must be accepted as well.

Suffering should not be promoted as a liberating and elevating summit at which we can join God. But let us not forget that the original meaning of suffering—to feel keenly—reveals the following irony: while feeling keenly opens us to suffering, it also opens us to the experience of joy, love, and beauty. This is why the incapacity for suffering, as well as the inability to bear grief and misfortune, is a serious moral and spiritual shortcoming. Philosophers like Hartmann argue that an incapacity for suffering lowers the value of human beings by leaving them weakened, disoriented, and even broken.

Hartmann's view was directed against the philosophy of the Stoics, for whom the primary goal in life is *apathia*, which means the absence of desire, even numbness and insensitivity. This insensitivity is in turn understood as a lack of *pathos*, as freedom from emotion. This is the life of no intensified feeling, either for the abundant experiences of the external life or for inner wealth. This is the life of closing oneself against everything that can awaken our desires and passions: the life of restraint and apathy. Since the world is too often not the way we hope it to be, since it is full of suffering and injustice, the Stoics argue that we can remedy our dissatisfaction with the world by blocking our dissatisfaction. They hope that by whittling down our passions to the point where nothing that is happening in the world can provoke them, we can gain peace of mind. If we get rid of the awareness "I am hurt," the Stoics think that we are thereby rid of the hurt itself. When we are protected against hurt in that way, outward things cannot touch the soul in the least degree. Despite endorsing the ideal of a wise man, the Stoic philosophy amounts not only to a mistrust of the world and renunciation of all human goods but also to a contempt for the noblest of them. The alleged virtue of the Stoics leads to impoverishment of life and amounts to ingratitude toward the world.

Hartmann was not speaking merely as a theoretical philosopher but as a human being who experienced significant suffering. He published his ethical theory in 1926, but he conceived of it while participating in War World I, the entirety of which he spent as a

German officer on the inhospitable Russian front. He was not there by accident. Hartmann was born in Riga, which then belonged to Russia. Since he was born in a family of Baltic Germans, Hartmann was raised bilingual. First educated in Russia, Hartmann eventually found his way to Marburg, where he received his degrees in philosophy. Unable to get a position in Germany, Hartmann returned to St. Petersburg where he became a Greek and Latin high-school teacher. He also married a Russian woman. Just when it looked like he was settled in Russia, he was invited to teach philosophy at the University of Marburg. Then the Great War broke out, and Hartmann was asked to retain one of his two citizenships and renounce the other. That is how he ended up on the Russian front in a German uniform, but it could easily have been the other way around.

During World War II, Hartmann was too old to be conscripted. At the outbreak of that war, he was a professor of philosophy in Berlin. While the war raged on, Hartmann continued to teach his classes until February of 1945, when the Allies' bombing of Berlin destroyed the university buildings and made further classes impossible. With his classes finally canceled, Hartmann turned to his long-delayed project of writing a book on aesthetics, the first draft of which he wrote between March and September of 1945. We do not have to be historians of that war to know how grim life was in the besieged Berlin of 1945, with the continuous aerial bombardment, the shortages of basic necessities of life, the Russian troops approaching from one side, and the Allied forces closing in from the other. In that living hell, Hartmann was writing a book that did not once mention war or destruction. Instead, his writing focused on beauty and sublimity, creativity and the meaning of life. This five-hundred-page masterpiece, written under such horrendous circumstances and during mind-boggling destruction of life, is an ode to the art of living and human creativity. How could Hartmann do that? Was he a monster, or a superman?

Whatever he was, when the first German universities reopened toward the end of 1945, Hartmann was cleared to teach by the Allies. He resumed his calling in the old university town of Göttingen, where he taught until he died in 1950. Hartmann believed that suffering is bearable when we suffer for something. A quiet and balanced soul, as he called what we would describe as a mature and wise human being, does not crave either happiness or pleasure. Nor does it run from suffering and pain. Such a soul recognizes the higher values, which Hartmann identified as spiritual and as part of the ideal being; it tries to realize as many of these ideals as possible, given external circumstances and internal predispositions.

Hartmann was not a particularly religious man. In fact, he considered himself to be an atheist. Nevertheless, he was religious in the broad sense of the word, which is better described as spiritual. We find a similar attitude in Viktor Frankl (1905-1997), a Holocaust survivor. Frankl was the author of the book *Man's Search for Meaning*, probably the most popular book on the meaning of life written in the last hundred years. At the time of his deportation to a concentration camp (in 1942), Frankl was a young, talented, and recently married Viennese psychiatrist. Based on his experience in the concentration camp, Frankl came to believe that having a reason for which to live is key to our handling of suffering. He became convinced that the way in which we accept our lives and the suffering they entail, the way in which we take up our cross, gives us ample opportunities—even under the most unfavorable circumstances—to add meaning to our life. Frankl argued that people in the camp died less from lack of food or medicine than from lack of hope. The forces we cannot control can limit us and deprive us of many things, except for one: our freedom to choose how we respond to what happens to us. Against many critics, Frankl admitted that it is true that very few people in the camp were capable of reaching such high moral and spiritual levels. He insisted, nevertheless, that one such example provides sufficient proof that a person's inner strength may raise him or her above their outward fate. Even if it was not possible for everyone to retain such a high degree of inner heroism at all times, some persons in the camp displayed a sufficient level of it. They were the ones who retained their personal integrity.

Most of us are familiar with a similar phenomenon from our own experience, even if the experience was less radical than what individuals like Frankl and Hartmann survived. In our age of intolerance of pain and anguish, there are, nevertheless, two types of situations in which most of us would readily cope with suffering. One occurs in the context of athletic (and artistic or similar) activities. Coaches push their athletes to their limits so that they can perform at their best during competitions. Good coaches make their athletes work harder and become more fit, confident, and better at what they do, but they also understand the individual gifts and limits of their athletes. They know that we each have an individual threshold for suffering; that threshold is different in every person and must be recognized and respected. Suffering can be of value only if this limit is not crossed. Once it is, we are crushed by any further effort. This is what Frankl witnessed repeatedly during his time in the concentration camp.

The second type of situation in which we do not resist suffering is when we are suffering for love's sake. A typical example is of a parent suffering for his or her child. Many stories illustrate how, under extreme circumstances, a parent can tolerate unimaginable suffering and complete a nearly impossible task just to bring a child to safety, take a child somewhere where they can be healed, or place a child in a situation where they can succeed—athletically, artistically, educationally, or otherwise.

We can analogously understand children's suffering for the sake of their parents, as well as the suffering of friends and lovers for each other. Frankl himself used his intense desire to see his recently wedded wife again and live with her for the rest of his life as his motivation to endure the humiliating and devastating obstacles of camp life. Unbeknown to him, his wife died in another camp, not long after his imprisonment.

Todorov on Male and Female Responses to the Camp Experience

After studying the moral experience of the Holocaust, the Bulgarian-French psychologist and philosopher Tzvetan Todorov (1939-2017) concluded that, on the whole, women survived the camps much better than men did. This is true not only in terms of sheer numbers but also in terms of psychological and moral well-being: women respond to bad luck significantly better than men do. Todorov offered two explanations for this discrepancy. The first is that, more often than not, with physical strength comes psychological weakness, and vice versa. Second, the psychological and moral makeups of men and women are different. Male relations are more confrontational, while female relations are more adoptive and oriented toward helping others. Men desire to display superiority and establish power over others. Women are left to heal the wounds that males inflict; they sympathize

> and care rather than dominate and conquer. Caring, according to Todorov, is the feminine virtue par excellence, versus the heroic virtues that are always attributed to males. Todorov maintained that the male psychological and moral makeup seems to be attracted to the concept of duty and the morality of principles (like the Ten Commandments), while women are naturally equipped with higher sensitivity and feelings of sympathy. He urged, however, that we do not forget that just as human biological life needs men and women to maintain itself, our social life requires the interaction of "masculine" and "feminine" virtues.

Such illustrations provide examples of deep commitments—to other persons and to the most important values. Certainly, they range from those extreme situations, which Frankl observed in the camp, to those more common situations, such as parents' love for their children. Regardless of the depth of suffering involved, these illustrations indicate that such suffering must have a significant impact on the meaningfulness of our lives. Suffering for a cause, provided that the cause is worthy, definitely contributes to a meaningful life. This may be the main reason why we use the phrase "meaningful suffering."

What makes us so afraid of suffering are the cases of meaningless suffering. We suspect that there are many more cases of suffering that is pointless than of suffering that is worth enduring. Bad luck is easily associated with meaningless suffering. In our time, millions have been infected with COVID-19, including those who are reasonably cautious about not becoming infected or infecting others. It is hard to imagine any reason why someone would behave carelessly and irresponsibly during a pandemic, but there are always plenty of those who do. By contrast, we can easily understand—and praise—those medical workers who expose themselves to sick patients every day because of their devotion to their calling. In a world in which so much is about money and pleasure, these medical workers work prolonged shifts, for days without rest, and are constantly in the vicinity of the infected. It defies reason to think that they endure the suffering they do for the sake of utility. Do we need any stronger evidence that sheer utility is not the most important motivator of human behavior? Or that there is an insurmountable gap between meaningful and meaningless suffering?

Meaningful versus Meaningless Suffering

One writer who dedicated much attention to the topic of meaningful and meaningless suffering was Dostoevsky (1821-1880). Good luck was rarely on his side. Dostoevsky was an oversensitive, sickly youth: a struggle with epilepsy made a significant impact on his entire life. Just as he was emerging as a budding young writer, he was arrested for alleged counterrevolutionary activities and sentenced to death. He was even led to the site of the execution with other prisoners, only to learn at the very last moment that, by the great mercy of the Tsar, their sentences were converted to years of imprisonment in Siberia. In his book, tellingly entitled *Notes from the House of the Dead*, Dostoevsky described many of his experiences in the Siberian prison, and they strongly resemble the memories of the survivors of the Holocaust. After ten years, Dostoevsky was allowed to return to St. Petersburg. He came back with a wife, whom he had met in Siberia. Unfortunately, she soon died of tuberculosis, leaving him with a grown son from her previous marriage, with whom he could never find a common interest.

Always struggling to make ends meet, Dostoevsky knew first-hand the excruciating poverty that he described in his works. In the rare periods when he had money, Dostoevsky could not resist the temptations of the roulette table. While dictating his novel, *The Gambler*, based on his personal experiences, he fell in love with his young helper, and they soon married. His second wife brought much-needed stability to his life. Despite his permanently fragile health and strenuous financial situation, fortune finally seemed to be on his side. But for every lucky experience, he experienced multiple bad ones. Their first child died only a few months after birth. Later, they lost another child, Alyosha, who died of the epilepsy inherited from his father. Dostoevsky was blessed, however, with two children who survived his premature death, at the age of fifty-nine. His life certainly resembled the turning of the wheel of fortune, but with far more time spent in the underground than up in the rarefied air.

Dostoevsky was preoccupied with the problem of meaningless suffering in connection with evil. Considering himself a realist, he could not avoid being aware of the overwhelming presence of evil in the world. Seeing the world through lenses that were sharpened by his personal suffering, Dostoevsky must have often wondered whether life was not only arbitrary but positively unfair, even pointless. Many of his heroes entertained thoughts of suicide, and some ended up committing it. Others could only accept that life is futile. In fact, in their view, life can be so twisted that we should wonder if $2 + 2$ does not equal 5. The "underground man," one of Dostoevsky's most memorable creations, could not live on the devastating surface of the earth but had to hide in its darkness. He could live, he said, as long as he could have his cup of tea, even if the rest of the world went to hell.

The underground man suffers because of the treatment he receives at work, the poor material conditions of his life, the bad luck of not finding a person to love and be loved by, a lack of passion for anything in particular, and a lack of faith in humanity or God. His defense mechanisms are designed to protect him against those misfortunes that befall him.

What happens, however, when those adversities are so deep that they affect every aspect of life?

Dostoevsky described one such case in the magnificent character Sonia, from *Crime and Punishment*. Sonia's father, Semyon Zakharovich Mermeladov, cannot resist spending every penny on alcohol. He loses his job and with it, the only way to support his family. The family's desperate situation drives Sonia to sell her body to provide whatever meager income she can. When Sonia befriends Raskolnikov, a few days after he has committed a double-murder, she realizes not only what he has done but that the depth of his suffering is far worse than her own. Modern man that he is, Raskolnikov mistrusts the world and lacks faith. Sonia, however, believes in a merciful God—despite everything. Irrational as it may be, this faith is so genuine that Sonia's soul remains pure despite the immorality of the means she chooses to provide support for her desolate family. While struggling to prevent her half-siblings from ending up on the street, Sonia falls in love with Raskolnikov and follows him to Siberia after he is sentenced to eight years for the murder of the two women. Both Sonia and Raskolnikov come to terms with their overstepping of boundaries, and they hope for a happier life together. Dostoevsky wants us to believe that their journey to Siberia is in fact their journey toward God.

Many of Dostoevsky's works were inspired by his hope of finding a convincing response to the problem of meaningless suffering. His last novel, *The Brothers Karamazov*, was the culmination of his creative effort and one of the greatest accomplishments of the human spirit. The story is, roughly, the following: Fyodor, the immoral and unscrupulous father of four brothers, ends up being murdered by one of the sons. Dmitry, the oldest son, is as passionate and unpredictable as his father; he falls in love with the same woman as his father and wants to kill him. Dmitry ponders what kind of father Fyodor is, while the reader is led to wonder whether we are better off with or without the Father in this crazy and pointless world. Because of his publicly repeated threats to kill Fyodor, Dmitry is accused of his father's murder and sentenced to twenty years in Siberia. But Smerdyakov, Fyodor's illegitimate son and long-time servant, has actually committed the murder, without regretting it. Smerdyakov is convinced that he was encouraged to kill the father by his half-brother Ivan, the smartest and most cultivated of the four brothers. Both a realist and a pessimist, Ivan is more deeply troubled by the overwhelming presence of evil and meaningless suffering than any other character in Dostoevsky's last novel. While realizing what he has done by inducing Smerdyakov to murder, and without being able to find any rational solution to the problem of meaningless suffering and evil, Ivan loses his mind. In addition to these three struggling brothers, there is also the youngest, Alyosha. Before the murder of their father, while their family is barely holding on (a symbolic reflection of the state of affairs in the wider world) the meek and gentle Alyosha tries to convince Ivan to affirm life. Alyosha urges Ivan to do so, despite the lack of rational reasons to live and all the unjustifiable evil and meaningless suffering. Love life, begs Alyosha, and only then will you understand its meaning.

Dostoevsky claimed in his correspondence that Alyosha represents his actual views. Many of Dostoevsky's acquaintances and readers suspected that it was Ivan who reflected Dostoevsky's deepest convictions, however. Ivan presented to Alyosha "The Legend of the Grand Inquisitor," which could be summed up as arguing that everything—including premeditated murder—is permissible in a God-less world. Ivan's Grand Inquisitor maintains that, in this world of ours, poorly arranged as it is, life is cruel and utterly meaningless. In this world, people cannot live off the idea of freedom and other ideals, as Jesus tried to convince them to do, for they would not only starve but also be continuously unhappy. Jesus overestimated both people's need for freedom and the significance of freedom. For the vast majority of people, freedom is an unbearable burden. They long to bow down and worship; they yearn for an object of devotion. Human beings need something more tangible than freedom to believe in, even if it is based on conscious lies and deceptions. The Grand Inquisitor's magnanimous goal is to make the lives of the small, downtrodden people bearable. His goal is to make them happy. Freedom and happiness are not compatible, the Grand Inquisitor insists, but illusions of freedom and happiness are. We can assume that what the Grand Inquisitor says about happiness holds for the meaning of life as well.

At the end of the Legend, Jesus simply kisses the old man and walks away. He has nothing to say to the old Inquisitor about his proposal to recreate creation, this time in the image of man. Dostoevsky did not explain why Jesus does not reproach the old man, nor why Jesus does not ask him how he imagines that he could make people happy. Did Dostoevsky think that a kiss, as a symbol of love, can give life meaning? Did he believe that the more capable we are of loving and of giving of ourselves, the more meaning there will be in our lives?

Like Jesus, Alyosha simply kisses his brother and hopes that Ivan can be saved through faith—if only his heart will awaken. But awaken for what exactly? For the invisible and just order that permeates the world, despite our eyes telling us that the world is fallen? Dostoevsky must have realized that, even if many human beings do not suffer meaninglessness because they are too occupied or too scared to think about it, some do. Could it be that it is precisely those few who ceaselessly search for the meaning of life who give meaning to humankind and are the best among us?

It is not easy to answer such questions. One reason for this is that Dostoevsky presented his views in an artistic form, rather than as a philosophical or theological treatise. According to the testimonies of those who knew him well, Dostoevsky's firm belief was that although we have to accept the existence of evil, if we give in to pessimism, whether in the form of resignation or self-delusion, life cannot have any meaning. In the face of evil and meaningless suffering, the only acceptable solution to the riddle of the meaning of life is that realism and optimism both have to be preserved. But how can that be possible?

There are a few solutions that are mentioned frequently in discussions concerning the meaning of life; they are believed to be strong enough to sustain our affirmative attitude, even in the face of evil. Without putting them in any order of preference, they are: renewed faith in God and trust in the world; love of life and love of other human beings; and flourishing, understood in terms of happiness and creativity. Frankl mentioned three different sources of meaning in life: work (in the sense of doing something significant), love (in terms of caring for another person), and courage to remain truthful to our pivotal values during difficult times (so that one's personal integrity can be preserved, despite unfavorable external circumstances). A sense of spiritual freedom and humor are also mentioned as the soul's resources in its search for the meaning of life. Such qualities are not always sharply delineated, and sometimes, they partially overlap. We will examine them in the following two chapters. For now, at the middle point of our journey, let us sum up what we have found so far.

Merit and luck are indeed important, and they contribute to finding meaning in life. But even bad luck, which in extreme cases could be debilitating, need not be decisive. Both merit and luck are external factors. Those that we just mentioned—from faith and trust to happiness and creativity—are internal. Rather than living like bouncing balls, kicked around by external events, we need to intensify our inner life and develop internal strength that can raise us above our outward fate, without making us numb to external events. Provided that we can do so, one question still remains: Can our internal qualities make our lives meaningful?

Chapter 3
Gratitude

The Crisis of Meaning

Our era is not conducive to living a meaningful life. Most of the institutions that are supposed to guide and guard our lives are not functioning well. In the best cases, they are inept; in the worst, they are corrupt. This holds for the whole spectrum of institutions, from legal and financial to political and religious, to those dealing with health and education. Trapped in the nets of such institutions, which deceive and exploit more than they help and lead, individuals are frustrated and disoriented.

Educational institutions play an especially troublesome role in our age. Institutions of higher learning are more concerned about their endowments than about the quality of teaching and the content of the curriculum. They have become corporations in which education is the product they sell, rather than the principal reason for their existence. This is true even for so-called liberal arts colleges, which are supposed to focus on broadening and deepening the cultural and moral vision of their students. Instead of helping them to discover sources of truth, goodness, and beauty in themselves, in their tradition, and in the world around them, such institutions are far more focused on preparing students for professional schools and highly paid jobs. Instead of introducing them to mastery in the art of living, such institutions instruct their students about the art of developing a marketable personality.

Even more alarming is that, by the time our children are ready to attend our best universities and liberal arts colleges, much damage has already been inflicted on them. It begins with the earlier stages of formal education and, of course, at home. Wonder and curiosity, together with spontaneity and playfulness, are the first victims of such education and upbringing, ensuring that our children are prepared "in good time" for the world of discipline and efficiency. The appreciation of beauty and the development of imagination are sacrificed together with any idealistic orientation, so that one day our children can function proficiently in the "real" world. In the course of our lives, however, we learn that being socially adjusted and successful does not have much to do with living a meaningful life. Nevertheless, as we ourselves harden, become artificial, cold-hearted, and often even downright cruel while chasing social accomplishments, we prepare our children for a world in which they will alternate between behaving like well-programmed robots (at work) and self-obsessed egoists (in their free time). By the time their formal educational process is over, little is left of the naturally ingrained sense of right and wrong, and even less is left of a sense of compassion and shame. What is left are human beings crippled for life, struggling to express, or even to feel, any subtle and genuine human emotions, and hardly capable of maintaining, or even establishing, any invigorating and lasting relationships.

Our grandparents, and in some cases even our parents, grew up with the mantra "work and save." Our mentality today is "work and spend." It dominates our profit and consumption-driven societies to such an extent that it makes us wonder whether this way of life is even compatible with leading a meaningful life. Our work obligations and social life leave us exhausted and stressed, temporarily entertained but starving for meaning. We behave as if the value of everything can be expressed in terms of market rates: we know the price of things but not their worth. Obsessed with monetary gains, we have become especially insensitive not only to the human cost that is paid to sustain this lifestyle but to the burden imposed on all life on this planet. We live in a world of spectacles, which allows us to "have fun" but corrupts our moral sentiments and discourages us from pursuing any deeper yearnings. One does not have to be clairvoyant to recognize the widespread symptoms of depression everywhere: from alcoholism, drug addiction, obesity, and gambling to minor criminality and frequent anxiety. Even the numbers and statistics with which we are familiar show that things are spinning out of control. In the most highly developed and wealthiest industrial countries, mental disorders and suicide rates are rampant, and the use of anti-depressants is at an all-time high and increasing. Prisons are filled to the brim, with new "correctional facilities" being built around the clock. How can we live meaningful lives when we no longer trust our institutions and when, socially and individually, things are barely functioning?

Reevaluation of Values

There is an important analogy between health and meaning in life. We think about our health when something goes wrong and then immediately deal with the problem. As soon as everything is "under control," we go back to living the same way we did before the problem occurred in the first place. Like health, the meaning of life deals far more with how we live and who we are in the long run than with the concrete choices that must be made and the specific actions that must be undertaken to satisfy them. Health and meaning in life are not to be taken for granted, for they are not simply given. They are aspirations we need to pursue: to replace imbalance with balance, to become and remain healthy, to lead meaningful lives.

The question of the meaning of life concerns our vision of life as a whole and our mastery of the art of living. Just as we can function on a daily basis when our health is not good, the mere fact that we are capable of handling what our lives bring to our immediate attention does not mean that we have mastered much of the art of living. In no art, including that of living, can we become skilled without much focus and discipline, sensitivity and awareness, knowledge and dedication. In ancient times, people assumed that we could master any art if only that art becomes the matter of our ultimate concern.

The ancient Greeks believed that the two greatest dangers in life were to believe in ideals that are not congruent with reality, and not to believe in any ideals at all. At the temple in Delphi, there were two inscriptions above the entrance that are still relevant for health and a meaningful life: "Know thyself" and "Nothing in excess." We are not good at either self-knowledge or self-control. They both require an honest grasp of our potential and our limitations, as well as persistent effort to live in accordance with such insights. To be able to do that, we need to become aware of our failures and shortcomings, as well as of our legitimate aspirations—both as human beings and as unique individuals. After we grasp such ideals, we need to assume their high points as our perspective on life and then remain under their continuous spell. There is nothing glamorous about such a demanding way of life, nor does it suit the spirit of our age.

Ours is the age of instantaneous information. We are capable of communicating with anyone anywhere in the world and of following any event that takes place anywhere on the globe. While this is a great achievement, it comes with a price: we confuse information with knowledge. Furthermore, the more we are informed about what is happening with anyone else, anywhere else, the less time and desire we have to understand ourselves: from our mounting anxieties and fears to our absent dreams and aspirations. The digital world imposes itself on us with such speed and such a demand for our attention that we become addicted to it and its "invaluable" services. We are connected to the global networks of information and reside in virtual worlds, while at the same time we grow detached from ourselves, as well as from the real and ideal worlds.

The technology that increasingly dominates our lives deepens the gap created by the tension between the principles of merit and luck. The former says that we are connected with all there is, especially the transcendent and divine core, in a way that is essential and inalienable. The latter says that we are alone, homeless strangers in a random and disconnected world. The former preaches that the world is more determined than it is; the latter implies that it is completely open-structured, which suggests that it is less determined than it is. While being informed about anything we can think of, we get caught in the gap of not knowing where we belong and how we should live.

Operating on the principle that more is always better, we are overwhelmed by endless sources of information. As a result, we tend to become indifferent and thoughtless. Arendt warned that thoughtlessness is one of the greatest maladies of our age, and there are plenty of reasons to agree with her. We avoid dealing with serious problems and are impatient for results. Nothing inspires us to walk the torturous path of thinking, which may not lead to any tangible outcome. Instead of engaging in serious soul searching and reflection, we hide behind historicism and relativism. If not historicism, then certainly relativism involves the rejection of critical and objective thinking. Arendt was convinced that our thoughtlessness ultimately leads to the abandonment of all high ideals and further moral degradation.

Jung on Four Functions of Consciousness

Carl Gustav Jung (1875-1961) noticed that while some persons favor thought as a guide for their judgments, others favor feelings; whereas some tend to experience the world through impressions made through the senses, others rely more upon intuiting potentialities, intentions, and similar partially hidden relationships. He characterized these four basic functions of the mind as follows: sensation tells us that something exists; thought tells us what it is; feeling tells us whether it is agreeable or not; and intuition tells us whence it comes from and where it is going. Sensation and intuition are irrational functions, whereas thought and feeling are rational functions. We cannot control sensations and intuitions; this may be more obvious in the case of sensation, but it is also the case with intuition. For example, insofar as intuition is a "hunch," it is not a voluntary act; it depends on different external or internal circumstances, rather than on a judgment. By a feeling, Jung did not mean an emotion (which is involuntary and irrational), but a rational evaluating function, which gives us a sense of joy, worth, and meaning in life. Jung's central insight, however, was that only one of these four functions dominates in the governance of a person's life, and it is seconded by one from the other pair of functions. For example, in most modern Western individuals, the dominant combination is that of thinking and sensation (with one or the other as the

> primary function), which leaves feeling and intuition in an inferior state: underdeveloped, neglected, or even repressed in the unconsciousness. Jung—as well as Hartmann—was predisposed to favor the functions of intuition and feeling.

Hartmann had a related but different view of the human predicament. Modern man is not prone to reflection and soul searching. He shies away from asking difficult questions, and the most important questions in life are those that are asked the least.

Nevertheless, Hartmann thought that an even more widespread problem of our age is our insensitivity toward the values that surround us, resulting in a general blindness with respect to values. In fact, we seem to have become equally blind both to the real and to the ideal worlds. Both worlds are indifferent about being known by us. But they reveal themselves to a great extent when we are open to them and grasp them to the best of our abilities—especially in terms of intuitions and feelings—rather than relying too heavily on sensations and abstract thought. Despite our firmly entrenched rationalistic prejudices, our knowledge of reality begins with our emotional reactions to the world, through which we first come to feel the hardness and rigidity of being.

When it comes to values, we are like starving people who do not see that the table in front of them is laden with food. Nietzsche's call for the reevaluation of all values ended up leading to the relativization of all values. Hartmann opposed this by arguing that values are absolute—and they can be so because they are ideal beings. As such, they can be intuitively grasped, even when they are not actualized in the real world. No less worrisome than the relativization of values is our inability to feel and discern values when they are actualized and part of the real world. This is why the most important ethical question is not what we ought to do, but how we can learn to observe the richness of the real world and participate in it.

The key point in doing so is that we need to learn how to face the world mindfully. It may sound surprising, but just as we often do not know how to listen to music or read books, we often are not very good at looking at the world. We usually have an interest in a narrow segment of being that is dictated by immediate needs. Coupled with an undeveloped taste for values, we then neglect multiple aspects of reality, not even suspecting what more may be there: even when we look, we seldom see.

A solution lies in perceiving the world with a sense of gratitude. Gratitude amounts to rendering the world spiritually significant by befriending it. An attitude of gratitude is aligned with the experience of centuries of spiritual traditions from the most diverse parts of the world. They all call for a change in perspective, for a transformation of the level of consciousness. Let us not behave as though we were nothing more than bouncing balls, kicked around by happenings in the world. Instead of approaching the world in a coarse and manipulative utilitarian way, let us allow the world to be what it is and accept it as such. To do that, we need to reconnect with the world by raising the level of our awareness and presence: to be mindful of the moment and place at which we are, not expecting anything and remaining open-minded about all that we may encounter. Let us delve below the surface of facts by feeling the vibrations of things and gaining insights into the deeper dimensions of reality. In addition to surface qualities, all things have their own "inner markings." Mencius explained what this means by pointing to a piece of jade. A master carver who wants to turn a piece of jade into a vase will respect those markings, or he will waste the piece of jade. With human beings, such markings remain regardless of what we experience in life. They are most visible when we are children, with little life experience, and when we reach old age, when experience has worn us down and revealed what is both essential and unique.

> ### Nepo on Giving and Getting Attention
>
> According to the poet Mark Nepo (1951-), giving attention amounts to seeing with a sense of gratitude, while getting attention is about being seen. Giving attention is connective; it awakens sensibilities in us and steers us toward the center of being. Getting

attention, by contrast, is isolating: it shifts attention away from other beings and toward ourselves. Nepo insisted on these distinctions because giving is more crucial to our health and overall well-being than getting. Giving attention is life-affirming; it is how we attend to things and connect to the world. Nepo also pointed out that giving and receiving do not exclude each other. In fact, giving of any kind initiates the dynamic cycle of giving and receiving, the greatest manifestation of which is a loving relationship in which giving and receiving are inseparable. Getting, which Nepo separated from receiving, is an addictive, one-sided attitude by means of which we try to fill our emptiness by having life come to us. Our yearning for approval drives us to be recognized; being seen temporarily relieves us of our fear of being insignificant. We want to be great rather than true, and we long for celebrity while secretly aching for something to celebrate.

Hartmann had similar insights and clarified them by distinguishing two fundamentally different ways of looking: "looking at something" and "looking through something." We are far better at looking at something: the world brings various objects to our attention, and we identify them. This kind of seeing is indispensable for practical tasks and is drilled into us throughout our education because looking at the world is the foundation for "navigating" the traffic of life.

Looking through something is what we struggle with. This is because we do not cultivate this kind of mindful awareness. There is an almost endless number of things we can see if we master the art of looking *through*, but many of them are of no practical use. I may notice how bright the sky is, that it has a peculiar "reddish" color that can be seen only in the early morning or after the sunset. Or I may notice that my daughter is going through her piano exercises with special zeal and attention to detail. Or that a slight change in my wife's hairstyle makes her look more beautiful. The experience of beauty, as well as experiences involving other aesthetic categories, can certainly contribute to our sense that life is meaningful. Ugliness and other negative aesthetical values lead, predictably, to the opposite experience.

There is a whole range of experiences that can make us feel that life is meaningful. We only need to recall the joy we have felt on many occasions while listening to a beautiful piece of music, or being astonished by the beauty of a landscape. Many such experiences are not moral, but they can have moral effects. They make the world seem ordered and purposeful, which always suggests a pattern that connects and a sense of meaning. This may be the reason why we are frequently prone to connect beauty and goodness and to relate both to a meaningful life.

We have similar feelings when we encounter an example of great nobility or extraordinary purity. But even something like a simple act of kindness may evoke a sense of meaningfulness. We recognize, for instance, the generosity of our neighbors, and even a touch of their magnanimity. When we pay attention to their behavior, we notice that there is something generous there that is extended not toward a particular person but toward everyone. We furthermore observe that what they do cannot be tied to any specific interests but reflects their "normal" way of life. Their behavior and attitudes are neither random nor based on any exchange of goods. Without expecting anything in return and without fulfilling any obligation, they seem genuinely to enjoy sharing and giving. They treat others with trust and kindness, with sincere intentions and open-mindedness. Their focus is on giving, rather than on getting. It is not that they would refuse a gift, or that they would not be grateful for it; rather, it is that they simply give, without expecting anything in return. They radiate with positive energy that seems to be contagious—at least to the point that, while observing them, we wonder how we can behave like that and become like them. It is hard to resist the impression that feelings and acts of gratitude enlarge us as human beings. Or we can simply say that they contribute something significant to a meaningful life.

Attention and Gratitude

We are in a very different territory here than when we are discussing the meaning of life in connection with merit and luck. With merit and luck, we are focused on the outside world and getting something from it: a reward for our virtuous actions or a lucky break as an answer to our needs or prayers. Looking through something helps us focus on what all too often escapes our attention. If our usual pace of life can be compared with riding in a car from home to work and back, imagine the same commute, through the same landscape, on a bicycle. Better yet, suppose that we transverse the same distance on foot. If we have ever done so, we were probably pleasantly surprised with what a different view we got of the same area. The familiar territory that we pass by twice a day suddenly reveals a wealth of details that escape us in the car. If we think of our car window as the frame around the picture we are watching, walking outdoors enables us to leave the frame behind and enter the picture itself. It makes us feel as if we are seeing something for the first time, as if our eyes are finally open. What we then recognize is that the world, down to its smallest details, which from our practical point of view may look very insignificant, is filled with surprises and treasures, unexhausted and inexhaustible.

Tagore on Two Approaches to a Journey

While discussing the relationship of the individual to the universe, the Indian poet, painter, composer, and philosopher Rabindranath Tagore (1861-1941) contrasted the Eastern and Western approaches to life. He distinguished two ways of looking upon the journey we undertake to reach a destination. We can look upon the journey as separating us from our destination and object of desire: seen in that light, the journey is an obstacle that we have to overcome, and we want it to be as short as possible. The second approach is to look at the journey as part of our goal: the journey itself is then accepted as the beginning of our attainment, rather than as an obstacle on our way. The first approach, which separates us from nature, is characteristic of the West; the second, which does not see nature as merely a tool with which to satisfy our desires, is characteristic of the East. Tagore's insightful illustration can also be used to challenge the distinction between means and ends and to argue in favor of an internal and appreciative approach to nature, as opposed to a more external and exploitative approach. Tagore insisted that until we relearn to experience nature as intimately connected with us and observe more directly, for no practical purpose, the sky above us and the trees and fields around us, we can hardly achieve closeness to our neighbors—or even to ourselves.

We will notice such a wealth of details only under one condition: if we care. To see the world as it is, we must care for it. The care I have in mind is that of active concern for the existence and well-being of other living beings, and for the world as a whole. Such care is focused on giving rather than on getting, and it is accompanied by experiencing joy through giving. It is by caring about things that the world becomes infused with meaning.

Understood in that sense, caring presupposes the presence of innocence and trust, of an almost childish approach to the wonders of the world. Mencius believed that a "great man" —or a person living a meaningful life—is someone who has not lost contact with his inner child. While there is a child in each of us that we must outgrow, there is also a child that we must preserve.

For four thousand years, the Chinese language has used the same word for heart and mind. The word *xin*, which we normally translate as heart, is more precisely rendered as heart-mind or, more elegantly, as the thinking heart—except that this could confuse us, Westerners, who are accustomed to the sharp separation of mind and heart, of thought and feeling. We translate *xin* as heart rather than mind because in the Chinese tradition, the focus is on human heartedness, rather than intelligence and reasoning, especially if they are understood in an abstract sense. Our intuitive perceptions of reality are far more reliable than our abstract concepts and theoretical constructs; such intuitive perceptions are not separable from feelings. For knowledge to be valuable, it has to relate to the heart.

We can again use Dostoevsky's characters as an illustration of this point. Raskolnikov's name means "schism" in Russian, and Dostoevsky plays with the meaning of the character's name by showing how Raskolnikov's heart and mind operate on different planes. Cold calculator though he is, having made a flawless plan to kill an old woman in cold blood, he cannot stand the suffering of Marmeladov's family and leaves them all the money he has just received from his mother, money that would have enabled him to have supported himself for a few months. Throughout the novel, Raskolnikov constantly fluctuates between his hatred of the world and his compassion for the suffering of humanity. He pushes Sonia away from him, claiming that he does not want to be loved by anyone, while yearning to be next to her. Sonia behaves quite differently, even in the face of the tragic events befalling her family. She never displays the ingratitude that characterizes much of Raskolnikov's conscious thinking and behavior; she does not lose her sense of gratitude. In some moments, while reading this novel, we may think that Sonia's trust and faith are delusional, but would not the same thoughts cross our minds if we were able to observe Viktor Frankl in a concentration camp or Hartmann writing his book on *Aesthetics* in the besieged Berlin? Gratitude may indeed border on the irrational and unbelievable, but this is because it makes us aware of the mystery of existence. It takes us beyond our categories of commonsense thinking, be they merit or luck, ends or means. If we come to recognize that gratitude is grounded in the recognition of what the world and human beings in it are really like, rather than on abstract thinking, we can accept it as ennobling and sublimating.

The Value of a Loving Gaze

Socrates and Plato considered wonder to be the beginning of all philosophy. Things that arouse our intellectual curiosity are novel things that usually have no profound consequences. Wonder, by contrast, deals with things that matter to us greatly. Since the word "philosophy" originally meant love of wisdom and since we can take Socrates—as Plato described him in his dialogues—to be the archetype of a philosopher who always had the issue of the meaning of life on his mind, let us recall how Socrates understood this expression "the meaning of life." Socrates led his dialogues, intending to help himself and his interlocutors achieve self-knowledge, by recognizing our legitimate and illegitimate aspirations. We are neither beasts nor gods, but who are we? And what does it mean to live a proper human life?

It is within this context that Socrates pursued his love of wisdom. He referred to that love as "Eros" and spoke about it metaphorically as some kind of semi-divine being. What he meant by it is that Eros is indeed something extraordinary, which cannot be accounted for through either the principle of merit or the principle of luck. The principle of merit does not require anything "erotic" of us: just to live properly, practice moral principles, and then be rewarded. A rigid adherent to the principle of merit may even be anti-erotic and overly pedantic by behaving as if life is a military camp. Such a person would believe that anything erotic distracts us from our duties and tempts us into sin.

The question of love is approached differently by an advocate of the principle of luck. At least initially, an adherent of this principle would be prone to connect love with luck: he or she would point out that we normally feel lucky to meet a person with whom we can fall in love, or unlucky that no such person has entered our lives.

Socrates was famous for insisting that he knew nothing at all, except for his own ignorance. Occasionally, however, he contradicted himself and said that Eros was the only subject of which he had knowledge. We should then pay attention to what Socrates had to say about it. For Socrates, Eros is neither a matter of luck nor a matter of worthiness. Nor does Eros refer to personal love; it is not love for any one person in particular—at least not in the sense of the love of Abelard and Heloise, Tristan and Isolde, or Romeo and Juliet. Eros is not a simple feeling but a complex set of emotions and attitudes, which include attention and care, admiration and a sense of relatedness; care and love are the necessary prerequisites for any genuine dialogue and interaction. There is one further element in Socrates' understanding of love that makes it very different from a Freudian instinctual impulse from below. For Socrates, Eros is not a push from below but a pull upward. As Socrates demonstrated through his relationships with his especially beautiful and gifted young friends—Alcibiades, as described in Plato's dialogue *Symposium*, and Phaedrus, in the dialogue with the same name—Eros is an affirming and loving attitude toward everything beautiful. Since Socrates believed that there is an intimate connection between beauty, truth, and goodness, Eros is a loving attitude toward everything that is genuinely valuable and thus worth loving. Following this view, Socrates maintained that philosophy consists of the education of our erotic desire in devotion to what makes us most human.

Like the rest of us, Socrates realized that there are many varieties of beautiful objects—from faces and bodies, music and speeches, to buildings and landscapes. What puzzled him was how it could be possible that such diverse objects, which have hardly anything in common, could all be considered beautiful. It is likely that Socrates never offered a definitive answer to this question, but such an answer was provided by his student, Plato. Plato postulated that there is something that he called beauty in itself: it is by partaking in this absolute and unchanging archetypal form of beauty that we can recognize the same quality of beauty in the most diverse objects. Plato thought that there must also exist other archetypal forms, for instance, those of goodness and truth, and that they represent not only the highest ideals but also the ultimate reality. The objects that we ordinarily consider beautiful and true and good are nothing but projected reflections and images on the walls of the cave in which we dwell.

When we speak of love, we usually think of it as a noun— "love" as a word for a person or object of our special admiration and desire. A bit less frequently but still often, we use "love" as a verb: what to do, and what not to do, to show our love in a proper way. Even less frequently, we refer to "love" by employing it in an adverb: there are certain persons and aspects of reality toward which we behave lovingly. This third sense of love is of the greatest significance for our discussion of gratitude. To see the world for what it is, to practice looking through it, we need to approach and see it with a caring and loving gaze. As the rays of the sun invite a rosebud to open its petals and release its scent, so a loving gaze invites the world to open its riches to us. Such a gaze establishes a bridge between us and the world. It creates an opening for us to recognize the thread of things, to enter the flow of life, and participate joyfully in its unfolding.

A loving gaze reveals to us that the world is neither fully determined, as the principle of merit tries to convince us, nor completely random, as the principle of luck suggests. Paradoxically, the world is both predetermined and underdetermined. If a rosebush is planted in fertile soil, gets enough sunshine and water, and receives the attention it needs from a gardener, it is likely to grow into a healthy plant and produce beautiful flowers. Alternatively, it could dry up or be eaten by animals, without ever reaching its potential. In that sense, there is not much difference between rosebushes and human beings. The dissimilarity consists in how many more factors there are, and how much more complex the factors are that determine whether the course of life will lead to full flourishing or degradation. If not in the life of a rose, then definitely in the life of every child, the most important factor influencing its growth is the presence and quality of the loving care it receives.

In general it is much easier to destroy than build, and this applies to living beings as well. It is difficult to grow a beautiful rose. Those who have tried know that it is far more challenging to rear a thriving child. Multiply the difficulty at least a few times—or should we, like Plato, say 729 times? — to grasp what may be needed for a human being to flourish and live a truly meaningful life. Socrates was well aware of how naïve many adults are about the difficulties involved in raising children, as witnessed by how many celebrated citizens—then as now—turn out to be inept at the task. Socrates considered that being able to foster that kind of flourishing—in ourselves and in others—is what wisdom is about; philosophers foster this flourishing by approaching the world lovingly.

The word "lovingly" indicates voluntariness, a voluntary approach. Such an approach is not a matter of luck—it is not accidental or indicative of a failure to do something. But neither does such an approach arise from any sense of duty—there is no obligation to become wise, just as there is no obligation to approach the world lovingly, become a grateful individual, or be healthy. This is an aspiration that aims at a rapport with the world, which in turn makes it easier for us to find our own place and role in life.

In pursuing wisdom, we should not overlook the fact that the world does not exist for us—individually or collectively. From the cosmic point of view, we are but a grain of dust in the infinite universe. Perhaps it is never easier to recognize that then when, far away from the city lights, we look at the starry skies and confront the immensity of the worlds above us. Paradoxically, at the same moment when we realize our cosmic insignificance, we can also grasp that we have been given the gift of being able to appreciate the richness of that universe and add something to it of our own, thereby making it even richer. Like an open book, the cosmos unfolds its secrets to our loving gaze and makes us not only admire what we see when we look *through* but also feel a sense of gratitude for the privilege of being part of it all.

Wisdom is grounded in our experience of the world and our self-knowledge. It is unlike our factual knowledge, however, for it does not deal with any specific aspect of the world, just as it does not predispose us toward any specific action. Wisdom deals with our understanding of life as a whole, which in turn instructs us in being, not doing. Wisdom is a way of being, a way of living, and a way of relating lovingly to whatever we confront in life.

Although one component of wisdom is intellectual understanding, this component is neither exclusive nor predominant. There can be no wisdom without what Mencius called the common heart and what Plato called the soul as a whole—which includes not only our minds but also our hearts and bodies. Furthermore, there can be no wisdom without our willing participation in the mysteries of life. Such participation is not active, in the sense of any direct action, but neither is it passive. It is a participation of affirmation and appreciation that involves calmness of mind and clarity of vision. It equally involves the capacity to love and the courage to hope that the highest values we grasp can be realized in this world.

A wise person comprehends that despite many differences among human beings—social and religious, cultural and individual—there are things that we have in common; these things pertain to our grasp of values and our living in accordance with them. The rudiments of a healthy grasp of values are present in all of us. Even to a person with a poorly cultivated moral sense, it is obvious that dignity is a higher value than personal gain, as well as that fulfilling our duty comes before the pursuit of pleasure. In all of us, there is conscience, which is a primal consciousness of values. Hartmann holds that conscience is a voice from the ideal world of values, a self-dependent and self-active power in human beings that is set apart from our will. As Dostoevsky illustrated the point in *Crime and Punishment,* conscience cannot be stifled by any utilitarian calculations of a positive outcome. Mencius referred to this idea of conscience as the common heart, while Socrates and Plato spoke about the human soul. Centuries later, first Blaise Pascal and then Max Scheler called it the moral "order of the heart." This order of the heart is in all of us, but it needs to be educated and cultivated. When it is fully refined, we call it wisdom.

Hartmann sometimes referred to wisdom by its Latin name—*sapientia*—which translates as "cultivated taste" and "moral taste." He thought of wisdom as a capacity directed toward our perception of the fullness of life and our affirming attitude toward everything that is of value. Wisdom is the penetration of the valuational sense into life, into every one of our perceptions and thoughts, actions and reactions. It is a morally colored spirituality that dominates every aspect of a person's life. As there is an undeniable difference between good taste and bad taste, there must also be a discernable difference between excellent and unrefined taste, especially when it pertains to values and ideals.

The central point of wisdom is to see the real world in light of values and ideals. A wise person lives not only grounded firmly in what he or she already knows of himself or herself but also in a span beyond. When the real world is approached in light of values and ideals, a developed "moral taste" enables us to exercise one of the most difficult capacities in life: ethical divination. The higher the values are on which we focus, the greater the perspective with which we can approach the concrete situations of life and plan our responses to them. Furthermore, the deeper the insight into the situation is, the more adequate our planned course of action. The loving and discerning glance of a wise person breaks through the boundaries of the ordinary and beholds the possibility of a different way of life, which in the real world is only intimated.

Let us clarify this by returning one more time to the comparison of health and a meaningful life. When we are healthy in the sense of having full integration and balanced functioning of our faculties, we feel a surplus of energy. Others may feel tired after working for several hours, or after playing chess or tennis for a while, but we are capable of going on with undiminished enthusiasm. The spiritual values, and meaning in life, are like a surplus in life, in comparison to that which is necessary for life's practical functioning. As indicated by the word *gratis*, a sense of gratitude is a surplus that is not needed for efficient or even successful functioning in life, and yet it enhances our entire life experience. It brings to life a unique quality of gratitude that would otherwise not be there. Furthermore, it carries with it a sense of measured optimism and hope that are not based on wishful thinking but on our being grounded in ourselves and in the world that surrounds us, as well as in a firm commitment to the highest spiritual values. When we experience life as meaningful in the sense described, it feels as if we stand with one foot firmly grounded in the real world, while our other foot is planted in the cloud of ideals and values. A meaningful life is one in which we balance our position between these two realms and integrate them into the same world, into the same life. It is a life in which we succeed in coordinating the real in light of the ideal.

Gratitude and Friendship

It is quite telling that we have developed vocabularies to deal with financial transactions and computer programming but are left searching for words when trying to understand the meaning of life. This is why I rely on a word that everyone can understand— gratitude. Let us compare it with merit and luck. There is, actually, a significant parallel between merit and gratitude. Both words describe stable qualities. If we feel gratitude—for being born in this world, for the gifts and opportunities we have received—it is going to be a more or less permanent part of our attitude toward the world and our lives in it. It is also a consistently positive and hopeful outlook. As the principle of merit reassures us that there is significant order and stability in the world, so does an attitude of gratitude. We feel that we belong to the world and have our place and role in it. Those feelings and attitudes are not based on the belief that the world is completely determined, or that it is thoroughly permeated by fairness and justice. The principle of merit reassures us: stay on the right side and you will be rewarded; cross the boundary of the permissible and you will be punished. Human life, however, knows no closure: it is not so straightforward, so linear, or so neatly ordered. As we all know, even when attempting to live as virtuously as possible, crossing boundaries and violating social and moral norms can teach us very important lessons that move us even more in the direction of justice and wisdom. There is no better way of learning than learning from our own mistakes and failures. As Hegel once put it, the fear of falling into error is itself an error.

We live in a world that is full of complex situations. We are frequently put in the position of having to choose among two (or more) positive values. Alternatively, we are forced to decide which of the unfavorable possibilities we face is the least negative one. The presence of such conflicts does not mean that our nature is sinful, or that every choice is equally valid. Nor does it mean that we should not have any preference at all, since every choice leads to an inevitable violation of some value. Choices have to be made, and we are responsible not only for making them but also for accepting their consequences. We have to face the world in a way that is both responsive and responsible.

It is precisely our inevitable participation in the complexities of life that should make us more appreciative—especially of those who strive to make the right decisions to the best of their abilities but nevertheless end up making the wrong choices. Such participation in the midst of life's conflicts creates an important sense of connection and unity in the world. This is not unity based on merit, fairness, or any theological conviction of the pre-established harmony between the world-soul (or God) and our soul. This unity is based on our acceptance and appreciation of what life brings, in good times and bad times. Taken in this sense, gratitude is quite different than luck. We are all eager to embrace whatever the wheel of fortune brings when it is in our favor—but not when it is not. The wisdom of various spiritual traditions teaches us to say "yes" to every aspect of life, to embrace it all. We are not able to cure the world of sorrows and injustices, but we can choose to straighten out our own lives and live in the world with joy and gratitude. If we can change the world at all, we can do it by changing ourselves, thereby contributing to the overall goodness in the world.

This may be the right moment to emphasize yet another point in which gratitude differs from both merit and luck. Somewhat surprisingly, both merit and luck permeate our competitive lifestyles and our deeply entrenched conviction that "the winner takes all." Whether we earn what we get, or are simply lucky this time, while fully aware that our luck could change very soon, we cherish our trophy and do our victory lap. Others can envy us or hate us, but this is our moment of glory. Gratitude is based on a different approach that is far more in tune with what we call wisdom. When we think of life in the course of our struggles, if we are sensitive enough to slow down and reflect upon the world and our lives in it, it is hard to avoid one realization: as much as earning and luck are important, there are gifts that we receive in life that we never quite earn. Moreover, there are gifts that not only are not deserved but which cannot be deserved no matter what we do or how lucky we may be.

Having intimate friends is a good example that illustrates this point. As Aristotle already recognized in *Nicomachean Ethics*, some friendships are mutually beneficial, and some exist for the sake of common pleasure. But there are also those friendships that exist for their own sake, and Aristotle was right that such friendships are among the most valuable things that we have in our lives. (Confucius similarly argued in the *Analects* that such friendships are divine gifts.)

Think about it for a second and test your intuitive reaction: if you knew a person who had never had an intimate friend in his or her life, would you think that this person had a meaningful life? Regardless of how morally upright this person's life was, or how much good luck this person may have had, it strikes us immediately that something fundamental was missing from this person's life. This missing element is so important that it presents this person's entire life in a negative light. A human being need not, like Sisyphus, be sentenced to rolling a rock uphill to live a meaningless life. Someone like Dostoevsky's "underground man," or Camus' "Stranger," may have enjoyed a semblance of a normal life, and yet a life spent without friends rightfully strikes us as pointless.

What is it about intimate friendships that makes them so valuable? What matters most in friendship is not what a friend does but who a friend is. More precisely, what a friend does is a faithful reflection of who a friend is. In some of the deepest and longest-lasting friendships, friends may not be able to see each other often, sometimes not for years. They need not attend each other's birthdays or other important anniversaries. They may not even know each other's birthdays, much less give expensive presents on those occasions. Nevertheless, when they get together, something clicks right away. The bond is so deep and the trust so complete that their appreciation of and gratitude for each other are overwhelming.

Gray on Camaraderie and Friendship

Reflecting on his experience in World War II, the philosopher J. Glenn Gray (1913-1977) pointed out that as long as we favor life over all else, we are not able to recognize how intolerable the burdens of our lives are. Put differently, the greater our obsession with survival, the less we care about the quality and meaning of our lives. Furthermore, the way we live, with violence and alienation permeating so many aspects of our behavior, is as if there is a veil in front of our eyes, preventing us from seeing what truly matters and makes us human. A decisive inner transformation, with an appropriate change of consciousness, would, according to Gray, include: an awakening, a coming to oneself, a discovery of friendship, and a falling in love. For him, these four seem to be various aspects of the same process rather than separate things. Gray particularly emphasized the role of what he called caring and concerned love, which he distinguished from ecstatic love, as exemplified in both sexually-oriented love and camaraderie. While ecstatic love breaks down the walls of self in order to merge with the other, caring love keeps them intact. Ecstatic love is impersonal; caring love is personal. Friends seek to understand and motivate each other, in an attempt to make each other complete, as they draw out the secrets of each other's being. When we have a friend, we do not feel accidental twists

> of fortune as much. Even during the most horrible experiences of war, the assurance of friendship has been enough to help warriors live through dreadful things without harming their integrity.

There is one further puzzling aspect of friendship. When Aristotle considered friendship among the greatest goods that can befall any human being, he was living in an age that, unlike ours, was not obsessed with the practical usefulness of things. Precisely because we are in our age, while we still readily admit the value of friendship, we have a hard time answering the question of what the use of friendship is. We can try to come up with answers, but all of them sound artificial. This is so because the value of friendship can hardly be appropriately evaluated in terms of utility. Friendship is not a means to anything. But in a world dominated by utility, it cannot be an end in itself either, for every end is also a means to something else.

Hartmann was not afraid to say that friendship has no practical value. More precisely, he said that friendship is a useless value. What is more, he argued that useless values are the highest values there are and that they are of paramount significance for a meaningful life. Useless does not mean futile or worthless. Nor does it deny the relevance of practical needs. The satisfaction of such needs sustains our existence, but it does not reveal meaning to us.

Useless values, especially as manifest in various forms of love, are the ones that bestow a sense of meaning on our lives. They make us experience our existence from a different perspective and stimulate us to keep going, to fly higher, and to strive toward life's most elevated peaks.

Living beings can exist and survive without spirit, but life reaches its zenith in spirit and through the realization of spiritual values. Among those useless spiritual values, Hartmann counted moral, cognitive, and aesthetic values. Together with love and friendship, gratitude is a useless value. So are personality and wisdom, truthfulness and trust. The presence of these values in our lives and our appreciation of them is what makes our lives meaningful in ways that are uniquely human. Neither gods nor beasts share them with us. Not even our supersmart iPods and computers!

Since love seems to be the most useless of all values, let us conclude this chapter by outlining Hartmann's view on the four forms of love: brotherly love, love of what is remote, radiant virtue, and personal love. (He did not specifically discuss friendship because he regarded it as a variation on personal love.) These forms of love are all spiritual values and should be understood as personal dispositions of affirmation. They lead to the development of personality and contribute to a meaningful life. Brotherly love is a form of spontaneous love directed toward those who live nearest to us; this form of love consists of a loving sense of another person's worth. As a value, love of the remote is higher than brotherly love, insofar as it consists of striving toward the humanely ideal. Love of what is remote is love of the worthiest and noblest, love of the creative spirit of humanity. Radiant virtue is the form of love that primarily refers to bestowing gifts. Personalities like Socrates and Jesus shine like gold and radiate virtue; they are people who, through the spiritual fulness that radiates through them, open the hearts and sharpen the eyes of others to the richness of life. Such individuals are living proof that an ideal can be realized in our imperfect world. Although radiant virtue can bestow meaning upon life, Hartmann believed that personal love is even more elevating insofar as it gives ultimate meaning to life. While radiant virtue spreads its gifts around indiscriminately, to all who are open-hearted to appreciate them, personal love directs itself to one unique individual and makes possible participation in the soul of another. It is hard not to agree with Hartmann that the penetrating spiritual intimacy of personal love is one of the greatest mysteries of the universe—perhaps the greatest one of all.

Chapter 4

Inspiration

Gratitude and Inspiration

There is an instructive medieval story about three hardworking stonemasons. Although engaged in an identical activity, to a traveler's question about what they are doing, they offered diverse answers. "I am sanding down this block of marble," the first said. "I am preparing a foundation," the second responded. "I am building a cathedral," the third announced. This story teaches us that remembering the greater cause of what we are doing is one of life's most important tasks—especially when the material we are working with is our own life. Human beings are not slaves of necessity, nor should they be slaves of utility. When we become so, we no longer recall why we do what we do. Losing that central focus on what matters most in life leads to an experience of monotonous routine and a meaningless life. Retaining a sense of the central vision guides our behavior, leading, by contrast, to the experience of meaningful life.

By using our medieval story, we can illustrate this difference as follows. Most days, and while doing daily chores, we feel we are just sanding down a block of marble—because that is what the present demands. On better days, when we are clearer about our grinding the stone, rather than the stone grinding us, we can do the same things but with a greater vision of why our activities matter: we are building a foundation for a sound and healthy life—our own or someone else's. On especially bright days, when our vision penetrates wider or deeper, our stone sanding least reminds us of Sisyphus' rolling of the rock; we dare to envision that the rock we are pushing to the top of the hill—or polishing with our hands—may become a component of something lasting and truly worthwhile. Whether it becomes a cathedral, a hospital, or a school matters less than the fact that our activities are directed toward enhancing and realizing an ideal of humanity. Such activities are performed by following our inspiration and by being an inspiration for others.

Just as there is significant variance in the ways we see the real world, there is a fundamental difference in the ways we reach toward the ideal world. Our believing may be bound by the factual and practical, based on personal evidence or evidence collected in our time. Alternatively, our believing may skip over the available evidence and point us toward the highest and greatest possibilities. In one case, believing is firmly attached to seeing; in the other, believing makes us see what has not been visible before. In one case, our goal may be balance and health, and in the other, it may be disturbance of the existing state of affairs and enhancement of human potential.

If the difference between gratitude and inspiration could be described in one sentence, it might be described like this: gratitude is about soul-caring, and inspiration is about soul-making. Or we can put it even more boldly: gratitude is loving what we do, and inspiration is doing what we love. A more subtle account would clarify both why gratitude and inspiration strike us as opposed to each other and how they also complement each other.

Gratitude means staying on the ground, retaining that broader vision, and feeling a sense of appreciation: for the presence of life, for its infinite richness, and for our being part of that astonishing and ever fluctuating river of life. Being part of something larger than ourselves enables us to realize that we should look for life's meaning not in pursuing our individual agendas and in isolation from others, but in participating in a "community" —social or cosmological—that we cherish as sacred.

Gratitude makes us balance life's various currents and contributes to an unperturbed flow of things. While being solidly grounded in reality, we need not worry about what tomorrow brings, nor whether the river in which we are but a minute part will find its way toward the all-encompassing ocean. Having a sense of gratitude toward life is certainly one of the greatest gifts that can be bestowed on any human being.

Inspiration is grounded more in intuiting what could be than in grasping what is. It is reliance on the power of imagination and the capacity to envision, rather than on self-knowledge and knowledge of the world; it is a shift in attention from the real to its ideal counterpart. This is what the Greek thinkers meant by directing us toward virtue. The original meaning of the word *arete*, which we translate as virtue, means excellence and virtuosity. Instead of being excellent athletes or coaches, students or teachers, or excellent in any other professional sense, Socrates wanted us to redirect our attention toward becoming excellent human beings. Our ideal, he insisted, should be virtuosity in the art of living. While we can say that gratitude aims at the meaning of life in a minimal sense—insofar as we accept and are grateful for what is—inspiration is based on a maximalist approach: What is the best that human beings can accomplish? Understood in that sense, meaning in life is as rare as it is difficult to achieve. Nevertheless, finding it stands above all other tasks as our highest aspiration.

Any symbolic representation of that highest ideal is treated as a manifestation of the sacred.

Inspiration calls for crossing boundaries and unsettling the existing order of things. Inspiration is not, however, rebellion for its own sake. It is a call for change that unsettles things before we can settle them again by establishing a novel point of focus, a new equilibrium. Like our search for health, inspiration is opposed to our practical need to merely adjust; it is motivated by our yearning for the ultimate sources of goodness, truth, and beauty.

The origin of the word "inspiration" goes back to the biblical tradition. To inspire originally meant to animate through the breath. According to the book of Genesis, God created the world by breathing spirit into inanimate matter. The breath of God animates things; it makes them alive. To inspire in the highest sense means to make most alive.

Inspiration and luck share some common features. Like luck, and unlike merit and gratitude, both of which are static, inspiration is a dynamic quality. Inspiration changes in its intensity and depth; it shifts in terms of the objective being pursued. They also share something of a dual nature: just as luck can be good or bad, inspiration can have two sides as well. We can be inspired by great and positive ideals or, alternatively, by evil designs that lead to the most inhuman actions: to destroy witches and heretics for the "greater glory of God," to cleanse the world of one race, religion, or ethnic group, or to infect a significant portion of an overpopulated world with a dangerous virus in order to create a more livable environment for those "truly worthy of living." The list of such sick ideas, which "Napoleons" — as Raskolnikov calls such powerful and daring individuals—are "inspired" to pursue, is long and not yet exhausted. Being inspired and creative means being able to shift the boundaries of the good and the acceptable—in the hope that better boundaries will be established, although there is always the risk of making things worse than they are.

At this point, we can notice a certain resemblance between inspiration and merit. In trying to earn what we can deservedly enjoy—a life of virtue and happiness, a meaningful life—we can control our effort but not its outcome. With inspiration, we dedicate ourselves to our ideals and embrace the breath that animates us without knowing where it will take us or how our adventure will end.

The principle of merit is straightforward with regard to how we are supposed to live and what outcome we should expect based on our actions. Things are less defined and more confusing when we consider inspiration: From where does the inspiration come? What exactly are we called to do? And how much should we be risking and sacrificing in the process? Let us shed more light on this complex and partially irrational subject.

Simmel on the Central Idea

The sociologist and philosopher Georg Simmel (1858-1918) argued that in every important cultural epoch one central idea is present. In an essay about the conflict in modern culture, he maintained that spiritual movements originate from this idea, and seem to be oriented toward it. Although each central idea is manifested and obscured in innumerable ways, it represents what he called the secret unifying and guiding force of the epoch. In every such epoch, the central idea resides at the point (or the center) at which the most perfect being joins with the highest values. To illustrate this insight, Simmel mentioned that the Christianity of the Middle Ages treated the idea of God as at once the source and goal of all reality, demanding devotion and obedience from us. Following the Renaissance, the focus shifted toward the idea of nature, and in the seventeenth century, it culminated in the idea of natural law. In the eighteenth century, according to Simmel, the center shifted yet again. This time, it was redirected toward the idea of the ego. In the form of human individuality, this ego appeared either as an absolute moral demand or as the metaphysical purpose of the world. In the second half of the nineteenth century, the idea of life was the central point: perceptions of reality were united with metaphysical and psychological,

> moral and aesthetic values. When Simmel was writing his essay (in 1914), it seemed to him that the contemporary culture had taken a decisively negative turn; unlike the humankind of the previous epochs, this one had no shared ideal and was without any ideal at all. It is worth thinking about whether our epoch is still drifting without any positive unifying orientation, or whether it is gradually beginning to lean toward a new central idea.

Some seventy-five years ago, Joseph Campbell made an interesting discovery. While studying myths from different parts of the world, he noticed one basic pattern that was repeated in them, with many variations. The pattern that these myths revealed was essentially the story of a life journey, told in terms of its central task: becoming a hero—or a heroine. It is as if each one of us is called to undertake an adventure to become a hero. Campbell published his findings in a book with a telling title: *The Hero with a Thousand Faces*. He described the hero's journey in terms of three stages: call, adventure, and return. At one point in our lives, usually during our youth but sometimes much later, we receive a call to a peculiar endeavor. It is as if the breath of God enters into us and calls us to leave the encircling shelter of the familiar world and embark on an uncertain voyage. To others who live with us, this sudden urge to leave the protective shelter looks irrational and impractical. And yet, something in us—which we do not fully comprehend—is stirred and cannot be easily pacified. We can refuse this call and continue with our usual way of life. Or we can accept it, cross the bridge that both connects and separates the familiar and the unfamiliar, and find ourselves on a lonely journey of trials. If we do so, we begin the second stage of the hero's journey. The trials are many and of varying levels of difficulty and complexity. Almost invariably, myths from disparate nations and separate ages agree about the greatest and most dangerous of them. It can be described as entering the darkness of the underworld and having to confront a dangerous dragon. There is no way around the beast. It must be slain, or it will feast on us. Symbolically speaking, the dragon represents the darkest and weakest element of our psyche, something that can make us our own worst enemy. To live from our own center, to become heroes, to mature and flourish in life, we have to confront that greatest weakness within ourselves and overcome it—or be defeated by it and brought under its tyranny for the rest of our lives.

If we succeed in defeating the dragon, we will find the treasure that the beast guards, and the treasure will be at our disposal. It matters less whether the treasure takes the form of a heap of gold or a fair maiden: if brave and crafty enough to defeat the dragon, we obtain the treasure we have dreamed of since our childhood days. Some heroes are tempted to stay with the newly found treasure and turn the hero's journey into an ego trip by establishing a paradise of their own. Regardless of how the paradise is described and what the treasure is, we still need to embark on the third stage of the hero's journey, for the journey must be completed: like the prodigal son—or daughter—we must return home.

Somewhat surprisingly, returning home with the treasure is the most difficult stage of the hero's journey. Think about the challenge it poses: we are coming back from a world that our relatives and friends, neighbors and countrymen, have never seen or sometimes even heard of. We are bringing home a treasure that is not of their world. In most cases, this treasure is not material but spiritual: a vigorous and inspiring vision of what human life can be like when it is at its best. Those who bring such treasures often become what Socrates called gadflies. Taken literally, the word refers to the annoying little insects that sting horses and cows when they are at pasture or resting and prod them to move, whether they like it or not. Symbolically speaking, gadflies are those individuals who make their societies aware of both what their ideals should be and how far they are from living in accordance with them. By making this discrepancy obvious, the gadflies provoke those around them to reexamine their moral standards and highest aspirations concerning what a meaningful life should be.

Such heroes and gadflies are saluted by some and feared by others. As in the biblical story of the prodigal son, for every welcoming father, there is a hostile older brother. What ends up happening to heroes and gadflies upon their return depends mostly on how powerful the forces are that defend the status quo and how threatened those forces feel by the new heroes and their vision. If the gadflies are not willing to make compromises or remain silent, or if their vision cannot be easily distorted or diluted, they are often sacrificed on the altar of the established and unforgiving gods: Socrates was sentenced to death, Jesus crucified, Bruno burned alive, and Gandhi and King assassinated. After their violent deaths, such individuals often become larger than life, with their adventures incorporated into new communal myths, into the new status quo. If we can disentangle their stories from the layers of fabrication that have turned their lives into spectacles, these individuals remain as inspirations and teach us values that are worthy of guiding our lives.

Campbell on the Heroine's Journey

Joseph Campbell (1904-1987) long struggled with one important question: Is there not a heroine's journey as well? And is it not different from a male hero's journey? After decades of deliberation, he realized that it is not easy to offer a fair and balanced presentation of both the similarities and differences of the hero's and heroine's journey. Traditionally speaking, woman is understood as the center of being, insofar as she resides in the realm of the hearth and home. Man's realm is the periphery, roaming around to catch prey and bring it home. In our age, the traditional roles of man and woman are blurring, which in many ways makes the journeys of the two sexes more similar than they were in the past. But some important differences remain regardless of such social fluctuations. Mythologically speaking, woman and man are symbolized as being and becoming: woman is; man acts. Woman is an embodied symbol of the mystery of life: she can give birth, and man cannot. The only thing man can do is serve life. Campbell reminded us that in many traditional societies, giving birth is considered a heroic deed. It is the giving over of oneself to the life of another, which may be the ultimate trial and perhaps the ultimate source—or matrix—of meaning in life. This act represents a unique form of transformation of life force, which is the point of every hero's and heroine's journey. Ultimately, Campbell held, it matters less how different male and female hero journeys are than that they create for each one of us the possibility of rapture in our experience of life: whether male or female, the central task of the hero's and heroine's journey is to identify one's individual bliss and follow it—until living from our own center enables us to recognize the radiance of one eternity through all perishable things.

The Upward Gaze

The key presupposition of the hero's journey is that there is something good in each one of us, as Mencius and Plato maintained so many centuries ago. This is not to say that everything about human beings is good and admirable. We certainly have a capacity for envy and hatred, violence and destruction; the circumstances of life and a lack of appropriate positive inspiration can push anyone in a negative direction. Nevertheless, we can turn in a positive direction and embark on our own hero's journey. Hartmann believed in what he called the basic law of humanity: from its primordial beginnings, the human race feels attracted to what is great and superior. We harbor within ourselves a persistent—even if sometimes thwarted—longing for something imposing and noble, and we search for it. When we find it, our heart goes out to meet it. Even when we spend much of our lives sanding marble, or engaging in any similarly monotonous tasks, when guided by a leading ideal, our lives can remain focused on central values and permeated by meaning.

We all need something to inspire us and lead us forward. Whether examples of greatness and nobility are provided by well-known historical figures, or by our internal grasp of values as part of ideal being, Hartmann called this approach the ethic of the upward gaze. Great individuals and the highest values direct our vision toward what it truly means to be a human being. These individuals and values instill in us the ideals of humanity and inspire us to realize such ideals in our own lives—to the extent that we can. More intuitively than consciously, in the secret depths of our hearts, we feel that those highest ideals are the source of something meaningful, inspiring us to live fulfilled lives. Everything great, claimed Hartmann, bestows meaning by itself.

From the time of the Axial Age until the era of the Enlightenment, such ideals have been represented as universal and equally binding for all human beings. In various religious doctrines, they are represented as unconditionally valid commandments and infallible dogmas. They tell us what to do, or what never to do, and we are expected to follow such commandments without contesting them. In secular ethics, the culmination of this view is expressed through Kant's categorical imperative: do your duty, as all rational beings should, regardless of your desires and fears, circumstances and social status.

Such precepts are so indifferent to our individual differences, as well as to how much the lives of people may have changed in the last two and a half thousand years, that many feel an irresistible urge to rebel against them. The rebellion has taken various forms and expressions, but for the last century and a half we have rejected the whole package of ideals associated with the Axial Age and the Enlightenment. We now emphasize nurture over nature, individual differences over our common essential characteristics, and subjective preferences over objectively valid judgments. This is how we have ended up in an age of relativism and disorientation. As the old saying goes, we have thrown out the baby with the bathwater.

Philosophers like Hartmann are so valuable at those crucial points precisely because they recognize that we have to navigate between the Scylla and Charybdis of absolutism and relativism. Hartmann, for example, realized that Kant's ethics is one of the greatest accomplishments ever achieved in the realm of philosophical thinking. Kant's insistence on a moral law and absolute values is to be fully respected, as must be his avowal that human beings should be treated as ends in themselves and never as means only. But there are points in which Kant was too dogmatic and insensitive to individual differences, to our emotions and intuitions, and to the imaginative and spiritual sides of our nature. Rather than reject it altogether, Hartmann reformulated Kant's categorical imperative to claim that we should never act merely according to a system of universal rules but always in accordance with the individual values of our own personal nature. Such an approach does not deny the importance of universal rules and values. Rather, it treats them as predispositions and recommendations and not as universal commandments and infallible dogmas. Hartmann's approach shifts the onus of moral thinking and judging from impersonal laws toward personal free choices and judgments in accordance with the values that inspire us. The question then becomes: Which of the conflicting values should I assign priority in any given situation, and which of them should I not? Free choice—and freedom in general—is both our greatest privilege and our most oppressive burden.

Following One's Bliss

Let us now relate Hartmann's reformulation of the categorical imperative to the meaning of life. To do so, we should return once more to the ideas of Campbell and the concept of the hero's journey. In his work with the students at Sarah Lawrence College, Campbell used a memorable phrase: follow your bliss. Many of his students, gifted and hardworking as they were, would come to him asking for advice about their life calling. What prompted them to do so was a familiar scenario: their parents expected them to follow well-trodden and socially respected paths regardless of whether those paths were leading those students toward becoming doctors or lawyers, businessmen or bankers. While the students were respectful of the wishes of their parents, they often had no predispositions to enter those professions. They wanted to become writers or philosophers or go into fields that few people were interested in and appreciative of, as Campbell himself had when he began studying mythology. Campbell would point out the distinction between calling and vocation on the one hand, and job and profession on the other, to his students. Against mainstream well-to-do society, Campbell advised his students to discover their ruling passion, the path of the heart, and to follow it, however unpopular or disrespected it might be. He reversed the famous words from the Gospel of Matthew that say: where your treasure is, your heart will also be. It is just the opposite, according to Campbell: where your heart is, there your treasure will be as well. The message is as simple as it is eternal: we find meaning in doing what we love, in living a life that we love.

While some students clearly sensed what their calling was, many others did not. Campbell thought that the central task of the whole educational process was to encourage students to get to know themselves through reflection on sources of truth, goodness, and beauty, and thus discover what path in life they were called to pursue. One's call is ultimately personal: it has to come from our internal recognition of what makes us most alive—of what makes us go on even when sleep-deprived and having to forgo many conveniences of life that others will not. The call has to be heard within and then embraced by the entire personality.

When we discover what our individual calling is, we need to embark on our hero's journey with full dedication to it. The tests awaiting us on such a journey will be twofold. Most obviously, they will be social and external: from our choices being condemned and even ridiculed, to experiencing personal rejection—whether from our acquaintances or our loved ones. We should not underestimate how formidable such obstacles can be. And this is related to the ultimate hurdle we will face when following our bliss: Will we be able to summon enough courage—time and again—to follow our bliss, regardless of the social obstacles that we continually encounter along the way?

If we are lucky, we may find helpers along the way. Campbell claimed that in his childhood, he was supported by his parents, who encouraged his interest in the traditions and customs of the American Indians, which interest soon expanded to include the traditions and mythologies of other nations and races. Later, he had the support of his wife, who he in turn supported while she embarked on her unorthodox calling as a modern dancer. Even though our hero's journey is uniquely our own, and not for any other individual to pursue, it helps to have a supportive hand, or to hear good advice, at key moments in our lives.

Campbell insisted that his life experience corroborated with a message he detected in many ancient myths: if the hero—or heroine—is pure of heart and has noble intentions, in the critical moments of the journey, the gods extend a helping hand. When we live from our own center and follow our bliss, unanticipated resources will turn out to be available just at those precarious points. In a secular context, we express the same insight by saying that luck follows the brave. Campbell had good reason to believe that it is not sheer luck that we are talking about here. What he had in mind we can clarify in the following way.

Recall again the principle of merit and the central insights of the Axial Age. If we work hard and live virtuously, the world is so arranged that there is a proportionate relationship between deserving and merit. The Axial Age understood the reasons for that relationship in terms of the pre-established harmony between the world soul and the individual soul. As this relationship is traditionally presented, it is, for the most part, one-way. Gods rarely intervene in our lives. We are expected to seek atonement with the gods, or the world soul, by following the precepts and commandments given. We can become like gods by imitating them.

Two fundamental issues with this approach are that it assumes that we know more about the gods—what they are like and what they like—than we actually do and that the line that separates good and evil is clear-cut and knowable to us. Notice that the emphasis is on us possessing knowledge—of gods and of good and evil—that we do not have. As Hartmann wisely added to these criticisms, we also do not choose between good and evil; we choose between two positive values or between two negative ones. He also called our attention to something that Campbell did not emphasize enough: the hero's journey has to consist in our pursuit of what we esteem to be the highest values. The journey must be about becoming the best we can be.

The phrase "becoming the best we can" seems to provide the most succinct answer to the question of the meaning of life. Let us thus make sure that we understand its message properly. The view that emerges from our considerations is the following. We need to cultivate our souls and grasp the ideal world of values as best we can. Then, in accordance with our individual gifts and predispositions, we have to follow the highest values whose call we can recognize within ourselves. Life is full of tensions and conflicts, and since it is a struggle, let us fight for the best and highest to which we are called. Engaging in this struggle to the best of our abilities is what makes life worth living.

Hartmann was less sure than Campbell about the role that gods—and divine forces—play in this process. They might play a role, yet they need not. And if they do play a role at some points, they may nevertheless leave us on our own at others. Even with the help of gods, nothing is guaranteed. There is no assurance that good intentions will be rewarded and lead to the desired results. Instead of any such promise, all that ultimately stands before us are our aspirations and inspirations: to become like those we admire and to strive toward the highest we can envision, in our own ways and with our own resources.

The life experiences and heroic journeys of those whom we admire teach us one more crucial point. Not only is the outcome of the journey not guaranteed, but the journey is worthless if we do not make it the central preoccupation of our lives—and treat it as if our lives depend on its accomplishment. When we enter the river of life and recognize the direction of its current, we have to follow it with all the concentration and perseverance we can gather. Otherwise, even if we are moving in the same direction as the current, we will be drifting rather than flowing. To live a meaningful life, not only must we discover in what our bliss consists, but we must also respond to what we discover with all the devotion we can muster.

My Inspirations: Albert Schweitzer

To illuminate these insights, I would like to share the stories of two individuals who have been sources of inspiration in my life: Albert Schweitzer and Antoni Gaudi. Their stories also illustrate how naïve it is to think that we either discover meaning or invent it. This issue is more subtle than that.

Albert Schweitzer (1875-1965) was born in Alsace, at the crossroads between Germany and France. He was fluent in both French and German, in addition to the dialect of German that only the people of Alsace speak. Perhaps that early experience, in combination with later living for decades in Africa, predisposed him to feel like a citizen of the world. Gifted at seemingly everything he touched, Schweitzer learned to play the organ as a child, and as a young man, he was already considered one of the leading organists in Europe. While still in his twenties, he defended doctoral dissertations in philosophy and theology, on Kant's philosophy of religion and the mystery of the kingdom of God, respectively, both of which he published as books. During the same decade, Schweitzer became the principal of the theological seminary in Strasbourg and a Lutheran pastor at the Church of St. Nicolas, in the same city. As if all these obligations and accomplishments were not enough, he was also preparing for publication the book that was soon to make him world famous, *The Quest of the Historical Jesus*. Hardly finding time to sleep while in pursuit of these diverse paths, Schweitzer received his hero's call, which, at least for the time being, stopped him in his diverging tracks. He recognized Jesus as his Master and decided to dedicate his life to following Him rather than to further pursuing his individual ambitions. Schweitzer believed that Jesus wanted him to serve the poor—the poorer the better. After reading some missionary newsletters, Schweitzer concluded that the poorest of the poor in his age lived in Africa.

Struggling with how best to answer his call, Schweitzer decided to enroll in a medical school, specialize in tropical medicine, then go to Africa to heal the natives. Against the advice of his relatives and friends, who thought that Schweitzer had gone mad, that is exactly what he did. His decision was supported by his friend Helene Bresslau, who was willing to accompany him on his journey. To do that, Helene requalified from being a teacher to being a nurse and also became his wife. On Good Friday, in 1913, the two of them embarked on their adventure, which, for Schweitzer, lasted fifty-two-years, until he died in 1965. They opened a hospital in one of the most malaria-infested parts of Africa, in today's Gabon, where there was no other doctor for a thousand miles. The hospital was located in the heart of the jungle and was accessible only via the river, on the banks of which it was located. The first decade was a terrible struggle, presenting them with one enormous problem after another. Finally, at the end of the 1920s, the hospital took off, and Schweitzer was able to attract enough doctors and nurses from various parts of the world to come and volunteer in the hospital. With his continuous publishing activity and frequent lecture and concert tours in Europe (and in 1949, in the US as well), Schweitzer generated enough attention to secure an unsteady but sufficient stream of medical supplies and food for the growing hospital.

Following Schweitzer's design, the hospital was more of a community than an institution. Everything in it that could be shared was shared, and everything that could be reused was recycled. All services in the hospital were offered for free to the patients and the families that accompanied them, but whoever was capable was expected to help with the work of the hospital in one capacity or another—carrying patients and cargo from the shore to the buildings, tending the garden and preparing food, washing sheets and ironing them. In addition to their regular work, the doctors and nurses were required to instruct the patients and their accompanying family members about hygiene and healthy lifestyles. On Sunday mornings, Schweitzer delivered a sermon for all who wished to attend, regardless of their religious orientation.

During his stay in Africa, Schweitzer coined a memorable phrase: "the brotherhood of all who bear the mark of pain." This was initially a reaction to the sense of guilt and the need for atonement which Schweitzer believed the white colonizers owed to the African people—and to those from other parts of the colonized world as well. Immediately upon his arrival, he could see the ill effects not only of slavery but of the massive spread of alcohol, firearms, and new diseases. The colonizers were all too often oblivious to the interests and well-being of the indigenous people. Colonization did not lead to their development but to their ruin. Schweitzer envisioned his hospital environment as a place where those trends would be reversed, for the natives were entitled to the same rights as the rest of the human race. He identified seven rights as the most important: the right to habitation, the right to circulate freely, the right to soil and its development and use, the right to free work and free exchange, the right to justice, the right to native organization, and the right to education. Listed like that, those rights seem a bit abstract. What is important, however, is that they are not primarily political or economic; rather, these rights deal with the creation of conditions that allow for the maintenance and enhancement of every human life. These are the ideals that Schweitzer not only proposed in the theoretical considerations of his ethics of reverence for life but also promoted in his hospital community.

Schweitzer's Ethics of Reverence for Life

There are six defining characteristics of the ethics of reverence for life. 1. Spirituality: this ethic has spiritual significance insofar as it seeks to attain harmony with the spirit of the universe. 2. Rationality: it is developed as a result of thinking about life. 3. Ideality: this ethic is ideal in a sense of being contrasted to that which is practicable and achievable. 4. Universality: it applies to all living beings. 5. Naturalness: this ethic is natural in the sense in which sympathy for the suffering of others is natural. 6. Ennoblement: it inspires sympathy as a natural disposition, the rudiments of which are displayed even by higher animals, and sympathy needs to be developed and ennobled in the direction of the highest spirituality. Schweitzer emphasized that

> reverence for life is a spiritual attitude that is the opposite of ruthlessness and thoughtlessness. We can weed a garden reverently or ruthlessly; we can even kill a poisonous snake reverently or ruthlessly, necessarily or unnecessarily. The principle of reverence for life does not demand that we be kind to our neighbor because this makes solidarity possible in society. Rather, this principle recommends that we be universally kind whenever the choice occurs. It does not dictate that it is a sin to pluck a flower or kill a moth. It recommends that we do not pluck flowers or kill moths without first greeting the divine principle in them and then only doing so as a last resort.

Schweitzer's selfless humanitarian work in the hospital, together with the increasing popularity of his ethics of reverence for life, earned him world fame and numerous awards. The greatest of them was the Nobel Peace Prize, which was awarded in 1952 but which because of his commitments in the hospital, he could not go to Sweden to accept until 1954. Faithful to his vision of service to others in the footsteps of Jesus, Schweitzer used the monetary award that came with the prize to build a leper village in the vicinity of the hospital and also to enlarge the number of hospital beds.

For most of his life, Schweitzer refused to be politically involved. Yet, the rapidly intensified nuclear testing in the 1950s and the growing threats of nuclear annihilation led Schweitzer to join the anti-nuclear war protests. His speeches, broadcast on the radio waves throughout the world, and his letters to the presidents of the United States and the Soviet Union, exhorting them to come to their senses and abolish all nuclear weapons and any further testing, turned him into a gadfly. His engagement provoked both worldwide support and a radically negative reaction in the West. A systematic campaign against Schweitzer was launched to tarnish his reputation. Various governmental agencies accused him of sympathizing with the communist regimes. Journalists were encouraged to write derogatory reports about the lack of professional standards in his hospital, as well as about his colonial attitudes toward the natives. Fame came at a price. Schweitzer tried to ignore both and worked in his hospital as long as he could. Luckily for him, he was able to do so until a few months before he died, at the age of ninety.

My Inspirations: Antoni Gaudi

Antoni Gaudi (1852-1926) lived a life no less dramatic than that of Schweitzer. There was no shortage of traumatic happenings around him: from the continuous tensions between religious conservatives and secular modernists to World War I and the Spanish Flu of 1918-20. Unlike Schweitzer,

Gaudi spent his life in his native land—Catalonia—rarely venturing outside of its borders. He even connected his understanding of originality in art to loyalty to one's tradition by insisting that originality derives from returning to the origin—both locally (the Catalan tradition) and universally (our primal closeness to and deep dependence on the divine).

Gaudi's life was organized around one single passion: architecture. He never married, dedicating his life to his work. From his thirties on, his circle of friends and collaborators narrowed, although there were always several of them who were deeply devoted to him. During the last decade of his life, Gaudi established his living quarters within the Sagrada Familia, the most ambitious project of his life; indeed, it is one of the most ambitious projects ever undertaken by human beings. Its foundation stone was laid in 1882, and it has not yet been completed. (The official website projects 2030 as the year of completion.) Although unfinished, it annually attracts more than three million visitors, who come to pay tribute to what is going to be—if it is not already—the tallest church in all of Christendom, and probably its most original and beautiful one as well.

One of the great challenges during Gaudi's own hero's journey was to resist some of the innovations that were being introduced to the arts. In our age, what an artist "creates" is intended to express the inner emotions and reactions of the artist, exactly as they are experienced, without much concern for what inspires such emotional reactions or for whether anything "out-there" in the world corresponds to them. Expressionism is the artistic movement that enthrones this shift; it is more radical than impressionism, which also conveys our impressions but only insofar as they are artistic reflections of an outside reality. As the continuous popularity of the works of Monet and Manet, Pissarro and Degas illustrate, quick movements of the brush, or dots in different colors put close to each other, create a pleasing impression. The works of expressionism do not please, nor are they intended to. They are more likely meant to puzzle, with their apparent disconnectedness and purposelessness. They create such effects because expressionist artists reject any "pattern that connects" the happenings in the outside and inside worlds. Like Nietzsche's rejection of outside norms and his shift toward life's internal impulses, expressionism merely reveals the inner emotions and reflections of an artist.

Gaudi was deeply disturbed by this approach to art. Surely, he maintained, we should not create impressions for the sake of impressions, or expressions for the sake of expressions. Why should that be considered art? Like propaganda, advertising, or entertainment, mere personal expression does not function as art. Proper art, insisted Gaudi, should direct us back to the deeper, foundational sources of our being, as well as toward the highest values to which we might aspire. He wanted to create art that inspires. Schweitzer reconnected with the source of being and the highest spiritual values by playing the religiously inspired cantatas of Bach, while Gaudi did so by working with stone. Both men were inspired by ideas and values that belong to archetypal images of the entire human race. They were convinced that the crucial concerns of their lives, and of humanity as a whole, did not depend on the latest fashions and technological inventions. Rather than perpetually trying to invent something new, we should trust that the past provides guidelines that we should follow. For Gaudi and Schweitzer, religion and art were intimately connected: both help us in our primordial quest for the meaning of life, but each generation has to reinterpret the clues for themselves, in their own ways.

Like Schweitzer, Gaudi combined conservativism and innovation. The Sagrada Familia has elements of medieval art, but it also looks futuristic. It both recognizes and defies the power of gravitation. The Sagrada Familia can be compared with the Taj Mahal or Hagia Sophia; like these two majestic buildings, the Sagrada Familia succeeds in finding the right balance between structural practicality and conceptual daring. The right balance is not based on any formula or law; instead, it is based on the right feeling. These monuments of art are not simple objects—or things,—nor should they be seen as such. Like living spiritual beings, they invite a spiritual, almost mystical interaction between themselves and the beholder.

Modern art, as well as the modern way of life, turns us increasingly toward reliance on artifacts. One of the main reasons why both Schweitzer and Gaudi have been such important sources of inspiration for me is because they relied on nature. Gaudi liked to emphasize what Leonardo da Vinci grasped at the very beginning of an era that involved an increasing reliance first on tools and then on machines for its achievements. Despite being fascinated with both nature and machines, da Vinci realized that decadence happens as soon as we forget to look at nature for our inspiration and seek to live in harmony with it.

In his youth, Gaudi was attracted to shapes we find in nature that we rarely examine or fully comprehend: conch shells, spider webs, and hexagonal honeycombs. In midlife, he was fascinated by the simplicity of an eggshell, which he used as a model for a few roof designs: an eggshell is one of the most fragile shapes we can find in nature, yet it is also one of the most perfect. In his later period, the shape of trees captured Gaudi's imagination even more. One of his inspirations for the Sagrada Familia was the cathedral in Strasbourg—started in 1015, completed in 1439—which was, for a long time, the tallest building in the Middle Ages. Gaudi perceived this cathedral as the sublimely towering, wide-spreading tree of God. He preserved and even intensified this symbolism in the Sagrada Familia.

Gaudi did this by creating a building skin that looks like crowns of trees, appearing solid from the outside but punctured from the inside and allowing the ethereal nature of divinity to penetrate the canopy via rays of light. Trees are deeply rooted in the earth, yet with their branches, they reach to the sky. They thus connect the underworld, with their roots deeply buried in the soil, the surface level of existence, with their trunk and lower branches, and the heavens, with their upper branches and tops reaching up toward the source of light. While designing the Sagrada Familia, Gaudi must have kept in mind not only the symbolism of trees but also the original meaning of the word "sanctuary." While for many of us, the first association of this word would be with a mysterious place in which divine energy is manifested, sanctuary originally referred to a circular space in the woods. When we walk through the Sagrada Familia, we feel as if we are walking through the woods, with the pillars shaped to resemble trees and rays of sun bursting through the stained glass windows the same way they would in the forest. In scenery like that, how can we not sense that we are encountering God's creation? And whether we are walking through the basilica or kneeling there in prayer, how can we not feel that we are in the continuous presence of God?

The Sagrada Familia reveals far more than just the inner emotions of its designer. As its name indicates, it is indeed a representation of the sacred family—in both its horizontal dimension, with the family members represented in stone on the portico, and its vertical dimension, which connects nature with God in such a way that we feel that every life is sacred. We do and must belong together, for we are all members of the Holy Family. While Schweitzer's sanctuary was his hospital compound in the jungle, Gaudi's sanctuary was the Sagrada Familia.

Understanding through Symbolic Language

Gaudi and Schweitzer met in Barcelona in 1905. The occasion for Schweitzer's visit was an organ concert that he was invited to give. In his autobiography, where we find a description of the meeting, Schweitzer says hardly anything about the concert but devotes two pages to his dialogue with Gaudi as they were standing in front of the Sagrada Familia. At that time, according to Schweitzer, only a portal, crowned with towers, had been completed. Like the great masters of the Middle Ages, Schweitzer comments, Gaudi began his work fully aware that it would take generations to complete it. The conversation between these two exceptional human beings must have been not only congenial but also profound. At one point, Gaudi was trying to explain to Schweitzer how the Sagrada Familia would incorporate the idea of the Holy Trinity. After struggling for a while Gaudi was so disappointed with his explanation, given in

German, that he suddenly turned to Schweitzer and asked him for permission to offer his explanation in Catalan. His excuse was that what he was trying to say could not be properly expressed in German, French, or English but that it could be expressed in his native Mediterranean language. Gaudi reassured him that only in that way, by listening to the explanation in a language in which he did not know a single word, would Schweitzer be able to comprehend what preoccupied his interlocutor.

The anecdote is quite revealing. Schweitzer did not present it as something funny, nor as an illustration of Gaudi's weirdness. It is certainly peculiar to insist on expressing an idea in a language that the listener does not understand, especially when you have at your disposal three other languages that he does. Nevertheless, in his autobiography, Schweitzer did not offer any indication that he was left clueless in front of his inspired host. Schweitzer's lack of any further comment rather indicates, I believe, his amazement that he was able to grasp what Gaudi was trying to make him understand. How could that be possible?

There are a few reasons for that. The first is that both men knew that our spoken (and written) language is only one means of communication—and perhaps far from the best one. Schweitzer could express a lot through music, while Gaudi could do it through the shapes, figures, and colors of stone. As gifted artists, they both knew that the language of symbols is more powerful than verbal language. While the main function of our verbal language is to refer and describe, the central role of symbolic language is to evoke. It calls our attention to something that cannot be represented directly but that can be intimated through the symbols used.

The second reason deals with the use of the whole body to deliver a message. While Gaudi was fluent in other languages, Catalan was the language in which he conceived the ideas he was trying to explain to Schweitzer. His entire body—including his eyes and hands—must have been more animated when he was speaking of something of such central importance to him, when he was able to express himself in his mother tongue. And Gaudi was probably sure that his gestures and overall body language would be invaluable in conveying his ideas in the best possible ways. (We can easily imagine an African patient of Schweitzer not speaking any of the colonial languages yet succeeding in explaining to the Great Doctor what ailed him or her.) The point is that, just as we can see much more when we care, so can we express and understand much more when we care. And just as seeing through something involves far more than registering the facts in front of us, so the expression of what we believe to the core of our being must be capable of being delivered and evoked better when it is done with our minds, hearts, and bodies all involved. Words are only social conventions; Gaudi and Schweitzer shared a conviction that below the surface of social conventions, we come face to face with something of a distinctive order of being that can never be properly expressed in words.

There is also a third reason. Both Gaudi and Schweitzer began their projects with no precise date of expected completion. In Schweitzer's case, the project was simply open-ended: healing people and helping them learn healthier ways of living. Gaudi was fairly sure that his basilica would not be completed during his lifetime. Their attitudes are analogous to becoming a loving human being and being centered on the highest values. When discussing love, we distinguished among love as a noun, verb, and adverb. As much as we would like to have an object of love—to love and to be loved by—it is more important to show our love through our behavior. Even more essential is to approach everything we do lovingly, regardless of whether such an attitude will lead to the desired reciprocal feelings, behavior, or outcomes. The Axial Age postulated that we need to be united with the highest being and the world as a whole. This highest being is often symbolically understood as the center: the source of life and the key to our orientation in reality. To be united with the highest being would then mean to live in the center—to become one with what is central.

While this noble ideal of the Axial Age appealed to Schweitzer and Gaudi, they both recognized that, as long as we live in the real world, a gap between the center and the periphery will almost always remain. Even when, in some moments, we succeed in overcoming the gap, we do not remain in the center. Our attention is diverted in a variety of ways and in multiple directions. What is important, and what is in our power, is to live in a way that enables us to remain centered on what is most sacred to us, on what is of the highest value. We cannot be continuously attuned to the highest and most sacred, but we should continuously strive toward it. It should always be our inspiration, the torch that shines for us and guides us in our daily challenges in the most honest and persistent way. Being inspired does not mean reaching our destination and uniting, once and for all, with the source of our being. Rather, it means staying centered on our destination throughout our life's journey, however far it may take us.

Inspiration and Meaning

Gaudi and Schweitzer's examples do not appeal to everyone. To expect that just this or that great person should be our inspiration—whether they be Gaudi or Schweitzer, Washington or Lincoln, Marie Curie or Mother Teresa, Tesla or Einstein, Tolstoy or Gandhi, or any other great individual—is to obscure an important point. What we are missing in our quest for meaningful lives is not inspiration from specific individuals and their unique heroic journeys. The key, rather, is that we be inspired by someone or something great and then remain centered on the ideals that are closest to us and of most concern in our lives. While we need not feel that we are at a sacred place when we attend Schweitzer's jungle hospital, or visit Gaudi's glorious basilica, what matters is that we find a place in which we each feel the presence of something inspirational. For can our lives be meaningful if we do not consider anything sacred?

There is another lesson to learn from such personal stories of life and creative efforts. While the insights of perennial philosophy are still relevant to us, achieving life's meaning is more complex than our great ancestors from the Axial Age realized. The values that lead to what we should follow in order to live meaningful lives are not pre-determined for us. What we are meant to be and how we are meant to live is neither pre-established, in the sense of some unavoidable destiny, nor something arbitrary, in the sense of a random individual choice. Values are equally independent not only of the will of human beings but also of the will of God. Neither God nor human beings make values; values make us, in the process of their realization. Our self-knowledge and our insights into the real and ideal worlds reveal to us that there is a net of indicators—signs and pointers—that are available to us if we are willing and ready to recognize them. Such indicators take into account both what it means to live as a human being and how we should live given our unique individual natures.

Our lives become meaningful when we are centered on such indicators and follow them to the best of our abilities.

Strictly speaking, life's meaning is neither discovered nor invented. It is a creative mediation between what could be and what is. The world as a whole is neither as it should be nor simply chaos, for otherwise values would not be realizable in it. The world is something in the middle: neither overdetermined nor undetermined. The world and our lives in it are underdetermined, which offers space for us to creatively contribute to life.

Living in accordance with the highest values amounts to a transformative mediation between what could be and what is. The realization of these values puts us in tune with the sources of truth, goodness, and beauty. When we center ourselves on the best and noblest, when we live our lives in such a way so as to enable truth, goodness, and beauty to be manifested in the realm of the real, we are then more than mere reflections of the world. We become a creative force that transforms in a double sense: we creatively transform both ourselves and the world around us.

However ephemeral our lives in this vast universe may be, when we live inspired by great individuals and the highest values, we do not need to worry whether our existence makes any difference. Nor do we need to ask then: Why are we here? When we become mediators between the ideal and the real worlds, the meaning of life simply pours in through the creative transformation of our lives and the world around us. We then love life and treat it as valuable, precisely because we are fully aware that there are things that we love and value more than life itself.

Closing Thoughts

We gathered in circles for thousands of years, as Wayne Muller reminded us. We gathered around fires, around bodies, around altars. Such circles, accompanied by rituals that were repeated until they became second nature, were sources of jubilation and consolation, of identity and meaning. The stories of old, heard countless times while we were gathered in such circles, told us what our ancestors valued and how we should live according to the same ideals. These stories made us believe that, as another poet phrased it, the universe is made of stories, not atoms.

The circles in which we gathered were connecting but also entangling. Each person knew his or her appointed place in the circle, regardless of what position the person may have coveted or warranted. Every circle provided a sense of security but also served as a chain that prevented much that was important from happening. And as it always happens, too much of one thing gradually makes it oppressive, and too little of another makes it desirable. After thousands of years, the ties that oriented us in our circle of identity and meaning became broken. The era of individualism—the era of self-made men and women—replaced the reign of collectivism. We can argue about when exactly that happened but, at least in the Western world, the era of individualism clearly dominated the second half of the millennium we just left behind us.

Our new millennium began full of premonitions. The individualistic mantra: "I can do it alone" has, in a matter of several centuries, come to feel problematic. Numbers do not lie, people say, and maybe we need no better gauge of the strain with which we are living now than to know the numbers of sick and dead from the present COVID-19 pandemic in various countries around the world. Where circles are enforced by unyielding leadership, the numbers of infected and dead are negligible. Where we do not gather in circles anymore, nor have a leader who can either dictate or inspire, the numbers are continuing to swell.

With the pandemic, as well as with a meaningful life, we have a few options. One is to continue embracing individual freedom and falling in ever greater numbers, at least until the pandemic runs its course. Another option is to persevere in our individual freedoms but rein them in with self-discipline and isolate ourselves from other human beings. Alternatively, we may come to realize, together with Wayne Muller, that we can do neither this nor many other important things in life alone. For how can we find any meaning in life when we are so disconnected from each other that only a few traces of our community circles are still visible? Must not any place that we rightfully call home be home to more than one person?

I used four qualities to describe how we can approach the puzzle of life's meaning: merit, luck, gratitude, and inspiration. Let me summarize what they are and how they relate to each other by continuing to use the metaphors of place. Briefly stated, merit can be compared with a workplace, luck with a marketplace, gratitude with a bridge, and inspiration with a sanctuary.

We spend too much of our lives in the workplace. If we do not count sleeping hours, the hours of our days are dominated by time at our workplace, just as what is happening on Wall Street may dominate our worries about the future. One positive thing about the COVID-19 pandemic is how it has revealed that much of what we need to do does not need to be performed within the constraints of the workplace; plenty of our work can be carried out just about anywhere. We can also see that the luck we crave is not limited to the unpredictably shifting numbers of financial institutions but depends on whom we contact and under what circumstances. Meeting other human beings and spending quality time with them, rather than crunching numbers, is far more meaningful, even when it includes the danger of infection: How else can we see a dear face, get a kind look, or hear a wise word? The fact that, despite all warnings and prohibitions, we all feel an irresistible need to gather together is indicative of how much life's meaning depends on human interactions and humane feelings. Somewhere deep down, we are still social creatures.

Somewhere deep down, the heart is more important than the head.

To be social and warm-hearted creatures, we need bridges that connect. I have in mind those bridges that not only physically join two places but are also elevated a bit in the middle. If not driving over, then certainly walking across such a bridge gives us a chance to take a good look at our environment and see it from a fresh perspective. It is good to pause on that elevated middle and survey what presents itself to our gaze without any practical pressure or preoccupation. A sympathetic gaze would easily discern the current of the water flowing below, the clouds rolling above, and the greenery stretching as far as the eyes can follow, for no reason or purpose. All of it is there "just so," as a Taoist sage might say. Just so, indeed, and yet our loving look at what there is makes us feel grateful that this cosmic dance is taking place and that we are part of it.

Such a panorama, whose pulse we can feel when we slow down enough to be with ourselves and our world for at least a short while, is a reminder that we may need yet another type of connection, yet another type of place. We need what we sometimes call a sacred place or sanctuary. What is sacred should not be identified with the holy, for it need not belong to or come from God. The sacred is what is set apart or consecrated, what should never be compromised or made profane. A sacred space could be any place—as long as it inspires, as long as it puts us in touch with something that motivates us to be true to what we value as the highest and purest, the noblest and the best. Traditionally, one such sacred place has been a church. Believers and parishioners attend churches in their most festive clothes, while displaying their best behavior. They leave their individual interests and differences behind and come together as a community: to share their joys and sorrows, to extend their helping hands to those less fortunate, to remember traditions and recenter their lives in the present, to be inspired by what is the most important and best in life. To live meaningful lives, we need to be able to trust, just as we need to have loving devotion for someone or something. To live meaningful lives, we must realize not only that we cannot do it alone but also that we must find a place where we feel at home.

We can respond to the sacred in a variety of ways. We can analyze it and dissect it with our powerful minds. Or we can accept it with our bodies as a manifestation of the divine. Most importantly, we can embrace it with our hearts. The more we think about it, the more we comprehend why Mencius emphasized our common heart and why, for Plato, the heart was the center of the soul. When it comes to the meaning of life, the heart is the center of our being, of our lives, and of our way of relating to everything that surrounds us. That heart that we all have—the same heart that we so often neglect or abuse, and which we should instead nourish and cultivate—is the key to a meaningful life. With that heart, we connect and appreciate, care and love. With that heart, we reveal our humanity and inspire each other to stand up after we stumble, to try harder, to strive to do better. Of all the circles in which we gather, the most important are the circles of the heart.

Further Reading

Arendt, Hannah. *The Human Condition*. Second edition. Chicago: The University of Chicago Press, 1998.

Aristotle. *Nicomachean Ethics*, trans. Roger Crisp. Second edition. Cambridge: Cambridge University Press, 2014.

Aurelius, Marcus. *Mediations*, trans. George Long. New York: Dover, 1997.

Campbell, Joseph. *The Hero with a Thousand Faces*. Princeton, NJ: Princeton University Press, 1973.

Camus, Albert. *The Myth of Sisyphus and Other Essays*, trans. Justin O'Brian. New York: Random House, 1955.

Eagleton, Terry. *The Meaning of Life: A Very Short Introduction*. New York: Oxford University Press, 2008.

Eliade, Mircea. *The Sacred and the Profane: The Nature of Religion*. New York: Harcourt Brace Jovanovich, 1959.

Frankl, Viktor. *Man's Search for Meaning*. New York: Washington Square Press, 1963.

Fromm, Erich. *The Art of Loving*. New York: Harper & Row, 1989.

Gray, J. Glenn. *The Warriors: Reflections on Men in Battle*. New York: Harcourt Brace, 1959.

Hartmann, Nicolai. *Aesthetics*, trans. Eugene Kelly. New York: De Gruyter, 2014.

Hartmann, Nicolai. *Ethics*, trans. Stanton Coit. 3 volumes. London: George Allen & Unwin, 1932. [Coit's translation was modified by A. M. Kinneging and republished by Transaction Publishers as three separate volumes: *Moral Phenomena* (2002), *Moral Values* (2003), and *Moral Freedom* (2004).]

Heschel, Abraham J. *Who is Man?* Stanford, CA: Stanford University Press, 1965.

Kant, Immanuel. *Foundations of the Metaphysics of Morals*, trans. Lewis White Beck. New York: Macmillan Publishing Company, 1959.

Lewis, C. S. *Mere Christianity*. New York: HarperOne, 2015.

Lin, Yutang, ed. *The Wisdom of China and India*. New York: Random House, 1942.

Mencius, trans. D. C. Lau. New York: Penguin Books, 1970.

Nepo, Mark. *The Exquisite Risk: Daring to Live an Authentic Life*. New York: Three Rivers Press, 2005.

Nietzsche, Friedrich. *Thus Spoke Zarathustra*, trans. R. J. Hollingdale. New York: Penguin Books, 1969.

Plato, *Collected Dialogues*, ed. Edith Hamilton and Huntington Cairns. Princeton, NJ: Princeton University Press, 1978.

Schweitzer, Albert. *Out of My Life and Thought*, trans. A. B. Lembke. Baltimore: Johns Hopkins University Press, 1998.

Smith, Emily Esfahani. *The Power of Meaning: Finding Fulfillment in a World Obsessed with Happiness*. New York: Broadway Books, 2017.

Tagore, Rabindranath. *Sadhana: The Realization of Life*. Radford, VA: Wilder Publications, 2008.

Tao Te Ching, trans. Charles Muller. New York: Barnes and Noble Classics, 2005.

Todorov, Tzvetan. *Facing the Extreme: Moral Life in the Concentration Camps*, trans. Arthur Denner and Abigail Pollak. New York: Henry Holt, 1997.

Quick Immersion Series

1. **De-Extinctions,** Carles Lalueza-Fox
2. **Populisms,** Carlos de la Torre
3. **Happiness,** Amitava Krishna Dutt and Benjamin Radcliff
4. **The Science of Cooking,** Claudi Mans
5. **Aristotle,** C.D.C. Reeve
6. **Jewish Culture,** Jess Olson
7. **Fascism,** Roger Griffin
8. **Nonviolence,** Andrew Fiala
9. **The French Revolution,** Jay M. Smith
10. **Jazz,** Joel Dinerstein
11. **The Cathedral of Notre-Dame of Paris,** Kevin D. Murphy
12. **Civil Rights,** Andrew Altman
13. **Feminism,** Noëlle McAfee
14. **International Migration,** Elżbieta M. Goździak
15. **The Meaning of Life,** Predrag Cicovacki

For more information, please follow us on Facebook @TibidaboPublishing or visit www.quickimmersions.com

www.ingramcontent.com/pod-product-compliance
Lightning Source LLC
Chambersburg PA
CBHW061651040426
42446CB00010B/1693